Murder & Crime
BOSTON

Murder & Crime

BOSTON

DOUGLAS WYNN

The
History
Press

First published 2010

The History Press
The Mill, Brimscombe Port
Stroud, Gloucestershire, GL5 2QG
www.thehistorypress.co.uk

Reprinted 2011

British Library Cataloguing in Publication Data.
A catalogue record for this book is available from the British Library.

ISBN 978 0 7524 5544 0

Typesetting and origination by The History Press
Printed in Great Britain

Contents

Acknowledgements

I would like to thank the staff at the Lincoln Central Library, the Boston Central Library and the Louth Library for their kind and helpful assistance. My grateful thanks are also due to Richard D'Arcy for his great help with the research and also to Ruth Gatenby for valuable information. Thanks also to Ged Payne for images from *The Illustrations Index* and to the editors of the *Boston Standard*, the *Louth Leader* and the *Grimsby Telegraph* for permission to use part of the publications under their control. I would particularly like to thank Nicola Guy at The History Press, for all her help during the writing of this book. And, as always, to Rosemary for her patience, help with research, driving and her constant support.

Introduction

A Short History of Boston

In Roman times the sea reached a lot further inland than it does today and the Wash was a much bigger area. Around the south-west corner of this arm of the sea, a line of higher ground gave rise to a series of small islands. When the sea retreated these became a curve, some 10-15ft above the surrounding Fens. This was breached by the River Witham, which ran on into the Wash. Where the river cut through is the port of Boston, situated at the nearest point to the sea where a bridge could be built. But at first, Boston was just a small settlement and part of the parish of the larger settlement of Skirbeck, which is mentioned in the Domesday Book. The early Middle Ages saw the port flourish. Most of the maritime trade was with the Continent and in 1205 Boston was the second largest port in Britain, after London. Boston soon attracted the attention of the Hanseatic League, a group of North German merchants, and some settled in the town to establish trading links. These merchants were sometimes known as 'Easterlings' or 'Esterlings' and it is said that the word 'sterling' derives from this because they were so honest and upright.

The loneliness of the medieval Fens appealed to the Cistercian Order, who established monasteries near Boston and Swineshead. They brought the cultivation of sheep with them, and soon wool was a major export, adding to the wealth of the town. The great Church of St Botolph's was built and Boston was known as St Botolph's Town, afterwards shortened to Boston. In addition to wool, salt and lead were exported and timber, wine and steel were imported. But even before the great church was finished in 1520, the town was in decline. The wool trade had largely petered out and the river was silting up, making it difficult for the larger ships to reach the town.

In the early seventeenth century Boston was largely Puritan in religion, but the religious oppression exercised by Charles I and his ministers caused many Puritans to flee the country and emigrate to North America. Several attempts were made to sail from Boston, only for them to be forestalled by the authorities. Afterwards a ship managed to sail from the Humber with emigrants to Holland, where they stayed for some years. Eventually around 250 people from Boston, including the vicar and many prominent citizens, sailed for America in 1630, landing in what is now New England. There, they founded the new town of Boston. Today there are strong links between the two towns and a major renovation of St Botolph's in the 1930s was largely paid for by the citizens of Boston, Massachusetts.

The fen country around Boston in the late seventeenth century was very different from today. It was low-lying with substantial areas underwater for a large part of the year and often covered in mist. Many schemes had been proposed over the years for the drainage of the Fens, but it wasn't until about 1630 that serious drainage began. Dykes were dug leading to small drains, which emptied into larger drains and ultimately into the River Witham and so on to the sea. Today the Fens still have the same pattern of long, straight waterways with roads often running along the banks. The Witham was straightened in the 1760s and the Grand Sluice was constructed at Boston. This reduced the risk of the Fens being flooded. With the drainage the soil improved and the Fens became much more productive. The subsequent increases in population in the country as a whole fuelled the demand for food and large areas of the Fens were used to raise cattle and sheep. Cereals and other arable crops soon came into the picture and areas were divided into new farms with rectangular fields edged with hawthorn hedges. Between 1800 and 1850 Boston became the largest town in Lincolnshire and the most active commercial centre, with more industrial activity than any other settlement.

But the coming of the railways brought disaster again to the port of Boston, since goods could now be moved about the country more quickly than by sea. But the railways brought their own employment. In 1848 the Great Northern Railway arrived in the town and eventually became the largest employer. There was a revival of the port in 1884 when the new dock opened. Larger ships could now reach the port and a fishing industry developed which survived until 1927. But commercial shipping continued to expand and the dock area increased in the southern part of the town.

New industries developed in the early twentieth century, including oil seed processing, food canning and other food processing, though many of these had disappeared by the end of the century. Yet the town today remains a vibrant entity, proud of its history and its links with North America.

Captain Swing

The early years of the nineteenth century were beset by agricultural unrest in the Fens. Returning servicemen from the war with France swelled the labour market and agricultural wages were very low. In addition, many farmers were bringing in the new threshing machines which put many workers out of employment, especially during the winter months when work was scarce anyway. The unrest showed itself in clandestine attacks on the new machines, the firing of stacks, threatening letters sent to farmers and even riots in towns and villages, where bakers' shops and butchers were raided because the rioters were short of food. The gangs were said to be led by a 'Captain Swing'. This was a mythical figure, like Ned Ludd of the Luddites. But he brought fear and terror to many farmers, especially those who lived on isolated farms far from the local fire engine, if there was one.

The attacks started in Kent and Sussex, but rapidly spread north to Cambridgeshire and the Fens around Boston. The first riot in Lincolnshire seems to have been in Stickford in November 1830 when a stackyard caught fire. This was quickly followed by fires at

Muckton and Ireby. Later on in the month a large fire destroyed a stackyard at South Reston, near Louth. Soon after there was a fire near Somercoates and then a wheat field was set on fire at Swaby. The rest of the year was full of fires at Sutton Marsh (near Long Sutton), Donington, Spilsby and Bourne. Many farmers began to give into wage demands and rewards were offered for information against the arsonists. Some authorities enrolled large numbers of special constables to try and patrol vulnerable areas.

Few people were caught but the attacks petered out in the spring and summer of 1831 when agricultural work became easier to obtain. However, those that were caught received heavy sentences. The heaviest fell on Thomas Mottley and Richard Cooling. On the night of 11 March 1831, a fire started at a farm in Lusby, between Horncastle and Spilsby. It destroyed a beast shed which contained a cart and some farming implements (it is not known if any beasts were killed). A stack of oat straw was also set alight. The owner of the farm was John Cherry, who lived a good ten miles away at Stickney, near Boston, but he was awoken at 3 a.m. to be told that his beast shed (referred to in the trial documents as a 'hovel') and the oat stack was on fire. He quickly organised a rescue operation but the building and the stack could not be saved. He then organised a search of the area with his employees and some neighbours, and the footmarks of two men were seen going away across some fields. These were followed and led to a house where Cooling's father lived. A search there produced some boots which were said to fit the tracks leading away from the fire. Richard Cooling lived at Stickford, near Boston, and the searchers went there and hauled him and his friend, Thomas Mottley, who lodged with him, out of bed. Accused of the crime, both rapidly put the blame on the other.

They were both tried at the Lincoln Assizes on 18 July 1831 before Mr Justice Littledale. Their defence contended that the so-called hovel did not constitute an outhouse as it was a separate building and therefore did not come within the compass of the law. And since part of the oat straw had been removed before the fire was set, that too did not constitute a stack. But the judge rejected both these submissions and the men were found guilty and sentenced to death. Mottley was also convicted of setting fire to two bean stacks and two haystacks at Stickford on 19 November 1830. Awaiting execution, Cooling never confessed, but Mottley did and told of several other stacks they had intended to burn. Cooling's father and his wife and child visited him the day before the execution, which was on Friday 29 July. Afterwards both bodies were buried in the Lucy Tower.

Chapter One

The Evils of Drink

'You're an old skinflint and a hypocrite to book!' shouted the Irishman. 'What does it matter if I have the occasional drink of ale?'

'I don't see why you need it. I can work just as well without drink.'

'Work? Work? You never did any work!' jeered the Irishman, whose name was Thomas Garry, although he was always known in the village as 'Irish Joe'. 'Why, when you went to plough you had to have a donkey to ride on. And when you got to the end of a row you had to get off the donkey to turn it round!' And with this final sally Thomas Garry turned his back on the other man, left the little cottage and tramped off over the fields.

The other man was John Newton, and he was seventy-four years old. At the time, February 1883, this was considered to be quite ancient. The Biblical term said three score years and ten, and he was beyond that. Indeed, John Newton himself thought he had reached the age when he might be expected to put his feet up. He had spent his entire life working the fields and for the last twenty-two years had been renting a smallholding of some thirteen acres from an absentee landowner who lived near Manchester. The holding was near Great Hale, a mile or two south of the larger village of Heckington, between Sleaford and Boston. John's wife had died some eight months before and he had come to the conclusion that he finally ought to give up the holding and go and live in lodgings on the money he had managed to save over the years. In those days there was no old age pension.

John Newton had a good reputation in the village. For forty years he had been a Primitive Methodist and a lay preacher, and he was a strict teetotaller. But he was known as a kind and generous man who would help anyone in difficulties. Since his wife had died he had taken in Thomas Garry, who had periodically worked for him on the smallholding, as a permanent lodger, giving him a small allowance but allowing him to live rent free in return for helping out in the cottage and on the smallholding.

Thomas Garry, the loquacious Irishman, was forty years old, 6ft in height, with sandy hair and a freckled face. Over the winter months, when there was little to do on the smallholding, he had been working for John Newton's son, Jarvis Newton, who was a carpenter and had a contract to repair the bridge over the South Forty Foot Drain at nearby Swineshead Bridge. Whether it was because he was now earning extra money, for labourers working on the bridge would earn more than a simple farm worker, or because he liked the company, we shall never know, but Thomas Garry had latterly taken

Great Hale High Street.

to spending more time in the Wheel Inn. This did not sit very well with John Newton, who would take every opportunity to urge temperance on others and they had several fallings-out about it.

It all came to a head on Wednesday, the last day of January 1883. That evening John had been preaching at a Blue Ribbon meeting of the Methodists, probably a Temperance gathering, in the village and he came home that night full of a certain exultation which religious people often have after a meeting or a service. Unfortunately, Thomas was late coming home and when he did he was drunk and aggressive. A furious row broke out between the two men and this continued the next morning after breakfast. Thomas eventually said that he was leaving and went off to work on the bridge. There he complained to his workmates bitterly about the sanctimonious old man with whom he was living.

John did some complaining himself. One of his neighbours was a young man called Edward Farmer. He was the foreman for a local farmer and it had been arranged that he would take over John Newton's smallholding when the old man left. Edward already kept a couple of pigs and some chickens there and he used to go and feed them every morning. He would normally chat with his elderly neighbour and they had become quite friendly. John told him all about the row he had had with Thomas that Thursday morning and the young man commiserated with him. Later that day, when Thomas had finished work, he came back for his evening meal. They ate their meal largely in silence, but after the meal Thomas said, 'I want my clothes.'

John's mouth turned down. 'We did say, didn't we, that the clothes were to remain as security for the money I lent you?'

'That's not very nice to bring that up.' He balled his fist and made a threatening gesture. 'Go and get my things. And if you don't do it, I will.'

But the old man, who by this time was trembling, was not to be bullied that far. 'If you want your clothes you'll have to get them yourself.'

Thomas stumped upstairs and John could hear him opening drawers above his head. Then the Irishman came down with a bundle of clothes under his arm and left the cottage without another word. He didn't come back that night, but spent it at the Wheel Inn. When Edward Farmer came to feed his livestock the next morning, the old man buttonholed him again. Plainly he was upset, but he also felt that he had been humiliated by the Irishman.

'I wish now that I had not let him have the clothes', he muttered. 'If I'd got a gun and stood in the doorway he couldn't have got past me.'

Edward patted the old man on the shoulder. 'You did right to let him have the clothes. You don't want to get into fights at your age.'

'Will you come and have tea with me tonight? I'm a bit lonely now that Irish Joe has gone.'

Edward could see that it wasn't because the old man was lonely that he wanted some company. Really he was frightened that the Irishman would come back and there would be further rows and possibly violence.

'Yes, all right, I'll come to tea.'

Edward arrived at about half past five that evening and John Newton had prepared quite a spread. While they were eating and afterwards, Edward let the old man talk. He kept going over what Thomas and he had said to each other; how the Irishman was ungrateful and unappreciative of all that he had done for him. This reminded Edward of the money he himself owned John and he duly paid him £1 3s 6d. Among the coins he gave him was a sovereign and he remembered afterwards that it had a flying horse embossed upon it.

Swineshead Bridge.

He tried to get the old man to talk about something else and questioned him about the plans he might have for his retirement, but he kept coming back to his quarrel with Thomas Garry. Eventually Edward said that he would have to leave. John pressed him to stay the night but Edward said he had to get back to his wife. Then John asked him if he would pray with him and the two men knelt on the floor while the old man said prayers. Then the young man left at about half past eight.

The next morning Edward was up bright and early and went to feed his pigs and chickens at John Newton's smallholding. He didn't see the old man about and when he had finished feeding his own livestock he noticed that Newton's own pig had not been fed. He went to the front door of the house to knock on it, but found that it was already open. Pushing it open further he stepped inside and called out, 'Are you not up yet?' But there was no reply.

The door opened directly into the living room and Edward saw John Newton lying on the floor. He was lying face up and the young man could see blood on his face and neck. Immediately he shut the floor and rushed outside looking for assistance. He saw a farmer called Mettam ploughing in a field not far away and rushed over to him. He told him what he had seen and asked him what to do. Mettam looked round and saw another farmer called Reid walking across one of his fields and both of them rushed over to him.

Reid was a more decisive character. He advised Edward to go for a doctor and told Mettam to fetch Jarvis Newton, John's son. The young farmer went to Dr Blasson and reported what he had discovered, then went on to the police station in Heckington and saw Sergeant Dennis. The sergeant and the doctor arrived at John Newton's cottage together. They discovered the body lying in a pool of blood. There was a fearful gash at his throat and they found an 8in butcher's knife on the floor near the body, covered in blood. There was also a severe injury in the left shoulder caused by a gunshot; nearby was a shotgun with one of the barrels discharged. The other still had a cartridge in it containing shot pellets similar to those found in the wound. At the post-mortem the next day the doctor found extensive bruising to the chest and he gave it as his opinion that the old man had first been knocked down by a blow or blows to the chest. Then, when he was on the floor, the assailant had made an attempt to cut his throat, finishing him off by a gunshot to the left shoulder. The sergeant found bloody footprints on the floor near the fireplace.

Superintendent Richdale from Sleaford was informed and he organised the investigation. After witnesses were interviewed it soon became obvious that Thomas Garry was the main suspect. It was discovered that he had not gone to work that Friday, but had spent the better part of the day drinking in various pubs in the district. By the end of the day he had become noticeably short of money and several witnesses testified that he had asked them for loans. He had left the Wheel Inn late that Friday night and most of the people there assumed that he was going home, but he had returned in the early hours of Saturday morning and stayed the rest of the night at the pub. The next morning he asked three people to say that he had never left the establishment the previous evening. He then paid for his board and lodgings and seemed to have plenty of money. It was afterwards found that among the coins he gave the landlord was a sovereign with the figure of a flying horse embossed upon it.

That Saturday morning Thomas Garry caught the early train at Swineshead Bridge Station to Boston. He spent the day there and returned by the evening train. He crossed

EXECUTION OF THE HALE FEN MURDERER

Thomas Garry, alias "Irish Joe," was executed on Monday morning last, within the precincts of Her Majesty's Prison at Lincoln, for the murder on the 2nd of February last, of John Newton, a small farmer, at Great Hale Fen Sleaford. The execution took place on the same scaffold as that used for Charles Anderson, the mariner who was executed three months ago for the murder of his wife at East Ferry. There were only officers representing the High Sheriff of the county and the prison officials present, the High Sheriff having declined to grant admission to reporters. During his incarceration Garry ate and slept well, and gained 17lbs. in weight. He did not receive visits from friends, his relatives being in Ireland—a sister and four brothers. He wrote to his sister, who sent a brief reply, hoping they would meet each other in the next world. He slept nearly the whole of Sunday, and until 6-30 on Monday morning. He ate a good breakfast, and then received the Sacrament at the hands of Canon Croft, Catholic priest, who has been most attentive to him from the passing of the sentence. Marwood entered the cell two or three minutes before nine o'clock and pinioned Garry, who bore up well to the last, but did not utter a word after the process of pinioning commenced. Marwood gave Garry a drop of eight feet. Death appeared instantaneous. Marwood said it was the smartest execution he had ever known. The black flag was hoisted on the clock tower. About fifty people being assembled outside the prison.

Garry did not make any public confession of crime, in fact it is understood that early in the morning he reasserted his innocence. He thanked Major Mackay, the governor, for the attention paid him, and expressed himself well pleased with the treatment he received.

The headline and a portion of the text from the *Louth & North Lincolnshire Advertiser* for 12 May 1883.

the bridge and went into the Plough public house. As the landlady served him she asked, 'Did you see my husband on the bridge?'

This apparently innocuous question seemed to startle Garry. He mumbled something inaudibly and then replied, 'Who's he looking for anyway?'

The landlady shrugged her shoulders and soon afterwards her husband returned. When he saw Garry he said, 'Do you know your master's dead?'

Garry shook his head and left quickly without finishing his beer. He next appeared in the Wheel Inn that same evening. The landlord here was more forthright when he saw Garry.

'You've done the old chap in haven't you?'

'Course I haven't!'

'You never did like him did you?'

'I'll tell you this though. The old b------'s worth as much dead as he ever was alive!'

The landlord nodded to a couple of men standing behind Garry and they quickly left the pub. A short while later they returned with Sergeant Dennis. He arrested Garry and

A view of East Heckington.

took him to the lock-up at Sleaford. When he was asked where he had been the previous evening he said that he had never left the pub all evening.

On Monday afternoon an inquest was held at the house of Mr Mettam. As was the usual practice, the jury were taken to John Newton's house to view the body, which was still there. The murdered man was formally identified by Jarvis Newton and Dr Blasson pointed out the injuries to the jury. He said that since John Newton's hands were not stained with blood it was very unlikely that he had killed himself. Afterwards, having heard from the witnesses, the jury brought in a verdict of wilful murder against Thomas Garry.

Garry was brought to trial at the Lincoln Assizes in April before Mr Justice Denham. The prosecution showed that the gun found by the body belonged to Garry and that marks in blood made by boots on the floor near John Newton's fireplace were identical to the pattern on the sole of Garry's boots, although no blood was actually found on the boots themselves. Witnesses gave evidence that he had left the Wheel Inn on the night of the murder and had asked people to say that he had been there all night. He was noticed to be short of money before the murder, but had plenty afterwards. The defence contended that the evidence was circumstantial and the witnesses were unreliable and prejudiced against him. But the jury took only an hour to find him guilty and the judge sentenced him to death. He interrupted the judge to say, 'I never did it, that is all I have to say.'

Thomas Garry was executed on Monday 7 May 1883. During his incarceration he put on 17lbs in weight. He received no visitors since his relations, a sister and four brothers, all lived in Ireland. He received the Sacrament from a Roman Catholic priest on the morning of the execution, but refused to make a public confession to the crime, and in fact reasserted his innocence. The execution was carried out in Lincoln Prison by William Marwood, the last execution he performed in Lincoln.

Chapter Two

━━◆◆◆◆━━

Beer and Skittles

They made a handsome couple. She was petite and pretty and he was tall and good-looking in a rough-hewn sort of way. She was Ann Louisa Favell and he was William Favell, and in the early part of August 1901 they were living in Bradshaw's Terrace in Skirbeck. Now a suburb of Boston, in those days Skirbeck was a hamlet just outside the town. And indeed, it has an older history than its larger neighbour, being mentioned in the Domesday Book whereas Boston is not. In the early 1900s it could be said that Skirbeck was the centre of the fishing industry, since many of the fishermen and the ancillary workers associated with the industry lived there with their families.

William Favell was a fisherman, an engineer on the steam trawler *Bostonian* owned by the Boston Deep Sea Fishing and Ice Co. The shipping company had been started in August 1885 with seven second-hand fishing smacks (sailing vessels), but soon acquired two new steam trawlers. The vessels were originally based at Hull, but when a new fish quay was built at Boston the vessels were transferred there. The company flourished during the 1890s and early 1900s, which was a boom time for the fishing industry in Lincolnshire and the East Coast generally. But in 1922 a collier, the steamship *Lockwood*, went aground across the Boston harbour mouth, completely blocking it. The vessel was eventually removed by the Boston Deep Sea Fishing Co., but because there was a dispute with the town council about payment for the work the owner, Fred Sparkes, took offence. He moved his ships to Grimsby and Fleetwood and that was virtually the end of deep-sea fishing in Boston.

William Favell was twenty-seven in August 1901. His parents also lived in Skirbeck, in Ashill Row. Ann Favell's parents, Mr and Mrs Earle, had a small grocers shop in Maddison's Row, which in those days ran from Freiston Road to Bargate Bridge and was only a minute's walk from the old church of Skirbeck. Ann was thirty-one. In her early twenties she had been a dressmaker at W.J. Crow's in Boston Market Place. Then she married Fred Palmer, who worked in the Ice Factory and they rented the house in Bradshaw's Terrace. They had one child, a little girl who was five years of age in August 1901. But Fred was killed when he was caught in the belts used to drive the shafts in the factory. Whether Ann received any compensation we do not know, but it seems likely that she kept the house on and took in lodgers. Again it seems reasonable that one of these was William Favell. It is reported that they lived together, co-habited was the term used at the time, for three years until they got married in January 1901.

Bradshaw's Terrace, Boston.

This seems to have been the crucial point in their relationship. Ann obviously wanted to get married. She had already had one child during her time with William and she was sure that she was going to have another. And although opinions of what constituted moral behaviour in fishing communities were perhaps somewhat different from those of the rest of the population, living in sin was still frowned upon. And a woman who did so was regarded as not much above a slut or a prostitute. But for William the prospect did not have the same appeal. He felt that he would be restricted, for a man who had another woman when he was married was an adulterer. But if he was not married, well, she was just another girlfriend. And this is shown by the fact that at the time of his marriage he was being sued by another woman, a Mrs Tredenick, for bastardy payments. At about this time Ann had saved up £23, which may not sound much but today would be worth about £2,000. The transaction was then worked out between them. William would take £20 and try to buy off the woman with that and then presumably he would agree to marry Ann.

At all events the marriage went ahead on 19 January 1901. But it soon became obvious that the situation did not suit William. Within a fortnight he began to treat Ann badly. Like many fishermen he drank heavily and he would often come home drunk and abusive. Sometimes he would not come at all, but would go and stay with his mother in Ashill Row after a fishing trip. The marriage tottered on until 9 August that year. It was a Friday and he hadn't arrived home again when Ann was expecting him, so she went out to look for him. She found him in Mainridge Road, but he wouldn't speak to her so she followed him home. When they arrived she asked him what he wanted for his supper and he said that he would as soon go to where he had had his tea than have his supper here. Needless

Ashill Row, Boston.

to say a row broke out between them. Eventually he left the house at about ten past eleven and went into the yard. She followed him out and saw that his mother was standing by the garden wall. Ann appealed to her, asking her to intercede. But his mother only replied, 'You're as bad as he is!'

At this William struck Ann in the face and she fell down. He then leaned down and grabbed her by her clothes and tried to drag her along the ground, muttering that he would have her blood when he got her inside. But Ann clung on to the gate and would not let go. After several attempts to free her hands and after his mother had pleaded with him to stop it, he finally let go. He turned and with a last few curses, saying that he would do for her one of these days, he went back into the house. While Ann cowered in the yard, William collected his clothes from inside the house and went off with his mother.

The next day Ann received a letter from him saying that she was not to send to the dock for his weekly wages as he had put a stop to it. It was common at the time for fishermen to be paid quite a low basic wage, but then to received 'poundage', which depended on the weight of fish caught. And it was also common for the basic wage to be paid to wives of fishermen if they were at sea. She wrote to him on 23 August asking him for support because of her children, but he came to the house in Bradshaw's Terrace early the next day and said he could do nothing for her. By this time Ann was becoming fed up with the situation and she consulted a solicitor. William was charged with desertion and the hearing before the local magistrates was scheduled for Wednesday 28 August.

The night before the hearing Ann was out in the village when William caught up with her at the corner of her street as she was returning home. He was drunk but not actually staggering about. He showed her a letter from Mrs Tredenick's solicitor saying that he was

Main Ridge, Boston.

to be summoned by her for non-payment of money towards his child. Ann and William were on the verge of another quarrel when he said that he would do nothing for either of them. He then showed her a revolver which he had in his pocket. Ann was appalled. Was the revolver meant for himself, Mrs Tredenick or for herself? She turned away and walked rapidly home.

The previous day, in the early afternoon, William had called at the premises of Messrs Slingsby Brothers, gunsmiths, in the High Street, Boston. After inspecting several pistols he eventually settled on a 7mm six-chambered pinfire revolver which he bought for 6s. He also bought fifty cartridges. When asked by Mr Slingsby what he wanted the revolver for, he said it was for protection. At that time it was by no means unusual for fishermen to carry guns when they went to sea, since they claimed that they needed them to protect themselves from foreign vessels. William repeated the assertion when later that day he went to see a friend of his, John Rason, who was a poultry dealer and lived nearby. He came to Rason's gate and showed him the revolver. 'I bought it for protection for myself. I haven't got a licence for it yet. I only got it today. I'll get a licence tomorrow.'

William wanted Rason to go for a drink with him. But the other man was uneasy. He could see that William had had a few before he met him and the way he was carrying on about his wife made him worried about the outcome. Eventually he agreed and they went to the Wellington Inn. After a few drinks William produced the gun and began waving it about, declaring, 'Four or five will be dead tomorrow.' But most of the habitués knew William as a braggart and seeing that he was well in his cups, they ignored him. Rason however asked William several times to let him take care of the gun, but William always refused. Rason went to bed that night a very worried man. Just as he was getting into bed

High Street, Boston.

he heard what he thought was a pistol shot. But the sound wasn't repeated and he went off to sleep. Early the following morning William came to his house again, and Rason again asked William to let him take care of the gun. Still the fisherman refused, but said, 'You can have it after today.'

The desertion charge was heard at the North Holland Sessions on Wednesday 28 August before the chairman, Mr T.C. Moore, and other magistrates. Mr W.H. Gane represented Ann. He briefly went through the facts of the case, pointing out that Ann was due to have another child soon and she was asking for a separation order.

'It's very early you know,' said the chairman of the magistrates. 'The complainant should have known the defendant's character at the time of the marriage.'

Mr Gane was somewhat shaken by the attitude of the magistrate and all he could say was, 'She thought it would be all right.'

'All that you've told me,' said the chairman, 'it wouldn't be of sufficient evidence in a divorce court, you know.'

Which really goes to show how difficult it was to get a divorce in those days. Apparently a man could have a child by another woman, beat his wife up, refuse to give her any money and threaten her with a revolver and it still didn't constitute grounds for a divorce.

But, again, all Mr Gane could say was, 'This is a more speedy way of getting her freedom.' Then Ann began to give evidence herself, answering questions by Mr Gane and with the chairman interrupting at times with questions of his own, such as, 'Was he drunk,' and 'Did he knock you down?'

At one point Ann protested, 'He told me to get my living on the streets!'

But William, who was in court to answer the charges, shouted, 'That is a lie!'

The Wellington Inn, Boston, now derelict.

The chairman finally said, 'Cannot you two people settle this? On 19 January 1901, you were married; you knew the character of the man before then. Don't you think you could come together again?'

'Yes,' replied Ann, 'or I should not have married him.'

'But now you have set out to end it.'

'I want to clear myself.'

Mrs Jane Wrack, a neighbour in Bradshaw's Terrace, gave evidence of the disturbance which took place on 9 August. She said she was downstairs when the row began, but she could hear it through the walls. After she went to bed she could hear it being continued. She got up and looked out of the window and distinctly heard William say, 'I declare I am dead to you after tonight. I will take your little blood. I will do it.'

But plainly the chairman was becoming tired of the arguments which were going on between Ann and William, and eventually he said, 'Cannot you settle this Mr Gane?'

'I cannot. She has had nothing from the defendant since 9 August.'

'She must take the rough with the smooth. It is not all beer and skittles.'

There was a consultation between the magistrates and then the chairman announced that they would adjourn the case for a week in the hope that reconciliation could be effected.

The hearing finished at about midday and later in the afternoon William went back to the gun shop in the High Street. He asked to be shown how to get the cartridges out as he could not turn the cylinder. He also said that one of the cartridges had fallen out the previous night and exploded. Mr Slingsby looked at William in a suspicious manner but he did not comment. He showed William again how to load and unload the revolver. Then he loaded the weapon for him, but warned him that he must be careful to keep the safety catch on. William thanked him and left the shop.

Meanwhile, Ann had left the Sessions House and gone to her mother's shop in Maddison's Row. At about a quarter to four that afternoon William arrived at the shop. He had obviously been drinking and was in a foul temper and he began abusing Ann and her mother. But Ann stood up for herself and another row began. In the middle of this a young man came in for some groceries and while Mrs Earle served him the other two went into a back room adjoining the shop. Mabel Earle, who was Ann's younger sister and who had been out in the back yard, heard the noise of shouting and came in through the kitchen and into the back room. When he saw her, William shouted, 'Clear off!' The young teenager stood for a moment, not knowing quite what to do, when Ann said quietly, 'Better do as he says, Mabel.' The young girl turned tail and left hurriedly.

Mrs Earle, having dealt with her customer, then came into the back room and hearing the argument still going on said to her daughter, 'Why don't you go into the kitchen, dear?'

'No you don't!' shouted William. He rushed over and stood against the kitchen door. And then, as if the sudden action had precipitated things, he pulled out the revolver and levelled it at the two women. The room was only small and he was standing only a few feet away when he fired. The first shot hit Ann in the chest and she crashed backwards against the wall and slid down to the floor. Further shots were fired and one hit Mrs Earle in the left arm. She screamed and rushed past him into the kitchen, where she met little Mabel coming in from the yard. William then seems to have stumbled out into the kitchen and eventually out into the yard at the back where he raised the gun and fired at his head next to a shed. Although he received a head wound he didn't even fall down, even though a huge pool of blood was afterwards found near the shed. He staggered back into the house. People were now rushing into the shop after hearing the shots. Whether it was because he saw the people coming into the shop and his escape cut off, or whether it had been his original intention, he stood by the body of his wife and putting the gun under his chin, fired again and fell dead at her feet.

The inquest was held the next day in the afternoon at the Napoleon Inn. As was the usual practice, the inquest jury were taken to see the bodies before they began their deliberations. The bodies were still lying where they had fallen in the house at Bradshaw's Terrace. Ann's was covered in a jacket and William's in a shawl.

There was an odd corollary at the end of this tragic tale. The coroner had originally sent his officers to engage St Nicholas School as a venue since it offered a reasonable space to accommodate the large numbers of press and public who wished to attend. But his request had been refused by the vicar and the school's headmistress on the grounds that it would bring disgrace on the school to hold such an inquest there. The coroner apologised to the jury about having to hold the inquest in such cramped conditions in the pub. But the jury had no difficulty in bringing in a verdict of wilful murder against William Favell and a verdict of *felo de se* (literally 'self murder') on himself.

Chapter Three

⇒◆⇐

Murderous Mother

The prison bell sang its mournful song and the clock stood at five minutes to twelve on that Friday in August. The procession formed at the door of the prison in the castle yard. At the front, a number of bailiffs stood with their wands. The chaplain, the Revd Mr Richier, was also in line with Mr Williams, the undersheriff, and Mr Hewitt, the castle surgeon. Captain Nicholson, the governor of the prison, took his place and he was followed by the executioner, William Calcraft. Behind came the prisoner, a slight woman wearing a black dress with a black bonnet. Two prison guards stood one on either side and close to her in case she should falter on her journey to the scaffold.

The little procession set off across the green sward towards the base of Cobb Hall. This medieval tower was built in the thirteenth century and still stands at one corner of the rough rectangle which constitutes the walls of Lincoln Castle. Inside the walls are also the assize court building, the Georgian prison building and the later Victorian prison building, the bath house or prison laundry and the Lucy Tower, the original motte of the castle. It was not a great distance, not more than 100yds or so, but twice the small woman faltered and would have fallen if the gaolers had not stepped in and held her upright. It was thus a slow procession which finally reached Cobb Hall. Inside, the prisoner mounted the spiral staircase to the roof of the tower with difficulty. Also on the roof were the governor, the chaplain, the castle surgeon, William Calcraft and the prison warders. At the time it was suggested in some newspapers that she could see from her cell window the erection of the gallows on the roof of Cobb Hall. It normally would have taken place on the day before the execution. But other reports claimed that Captain Nicholson did not arrange for the gallows to be put up until 5 a.m. on the Friday, the day of the execution.

In those days executions were carried out in public and in Lincoln they were usually arranged for a market day to ensure a substantial crowd, for the execution could be seen from the streets below the castle walls. And on this particular Friday, the area outside the walls and every street giving a view of the top of Cobb Hall was crowded with men, women and even children, while hawkers moved among them trying to sell their wares.

The prisoner was assisted up the steps of the gallows and faced the immense crowd below. A silence descended and the chaplain standing at the bottom of the steps of the gallows began to read part of the burial service. The woman took one last look around as the executioner removed her bonnet. He then tied her hands in front of her and put a white cap over her head, shutting out the sight of the world around her for the last time.

A full, true, and particular account of the Life, Trial, Confession, and Execution of

ELIZA JOYCE, Aged 31,

Who was Executed on the Drop at Lincoln, on Friday, August 2nd, 1844, for Poisoning Emma and Ann Joyce, her daughters.

At the Lincoln Assizes, on Monday 22 July 1844 Eliza Joyce, aged 31, a mild and not uninteresting-looking woman, the wife of a gardener, at Boston was arraigned upon, and pleaded guilty to, two indictments, charging her with the crime of wilful murder. The first indictment charged the murdering by poison (laudanum) in the month of October, 1841, of Emma Joyce, aged 18 months, the child of her husband by a former marriage, The second indictment charged the murdering by poison (laudanum) in the month of January, 1842, of Ann Joyce, aged six weeks, her own offspring by her marriage. The unhappy being was arraigned at the Spring Assizes last year upon the charge of administering to Edward William Joyce (a child of her husband's, of some years' growth) arsenic, whereby his death was caused, and to that indictment pleaded not guilty, and thereon, in consequence of proof to the name of William only, and not of Edward William, being offered, she was discharged, sureties being taken for her trial at the then next ensuing Summer Assizes. She was again arraigned thereon at the Summer Assizs of last year, and acquitted As will be seen by her confession below, she now admitted the murder of the said Edward William Joyce, as well as the murders (all at different times) of Emma Joyce and Ann Joyce.

The shocking scene lasted but a very few minutes. The wretched creature only faintly uttered on each arraignment, "I am guilty," and the Judge performed his sad duty in as few words and as short a time as decency and the observance of customary from would permit.

The following evidence was given before Mr. John Sturdy, Mayor of Boston, which embodies her confession on which she was committed.

Edward Coupland, of Boston, surgeon, was one of the medical officers of the Boston Poor Law Union. He had attended Mrs. Joyce, one of the inmates of the said Union, during her illness. On Monday the 1st of July, instant, he visited Eliza Joyce as usual, and in her conversation with him she alluded to the circumstance of the death of Mr. Joyce's son William, a boy about 15 years of age, and at the same time stated that she had admin-

istered arsenic to him. He then asked her how much? She replied, "About a teaspoonful." He then went on conversing with her relative to the child three weeks old, and another little girl called Emma, observing that in the surgical examination of the body of the latter, which was exhumed for that purpose, he could not detect any arsenic. She then said, "Oh no, sir, I did not give her arsenic; I gave her laudanum." He then asked if she had given anything to the other child. She replied, "Yes: I also gave it laudanum." Witness then said, "How much do you think you gave each? She replied, "About a teaspoonful to the baby, and about two tea-spoonsful to the little girl Emma;" but in a conversation he had with her on the following day, she stated that she gave two spoonfulls to the baby, and about four tea-spoonfuls to the girl Emma. Witness then asked her how much she had purchased. She replied "three-pennyworth" and that she obtained it at Mr. Smith's shop in Boston. Witness was the surgeon who examined the body of Emma Joyce, the daughter of William, after exhumation, owing to a suspicion that arsenic had been administered to it; but on fully testing the contents of the stomach, and the parts immediately around it, he came to the conclusion that arsenic had not been administered. The child had been interred several months.

The woman having been sentenced to suffer death as above stated, tranquilly suffered herself to be removed from the bar.

Since her conviction the unfortunate woman has behaved in a manner befitting her in her dreadful situation, she has paid every attention to the spiritual instruction of the worthy chaplin.

On Thursday afternoon the condemned sermon was preached by the Rev. Mr. Ritchter, chaplain to the castle, the discourse was impressive, and appeared to have considerable effect not only on the wretched woman but on the whole of prisoners present.

At the appointed hour, this day, the unfortunate culprit was conducted to the Drop, on the Castle walls, and underwent the sentence her crimes so justly merited, in the presence of an immense concourse of spectators.

A Copy of Verses.

Alas my heart was blinded then,
By Satan's powerful sway;
That dreadful enemy of men
My reason took away.

I saw not then the dismal cell,
The Judge or Judgment seat;
The place where crime is doom'd to dwell
And there its deserts meet.

Hark I hear the prison door,
On its grating hinges turn,
A few sad mournful moments more,
And I'm for ever gone.

Hark the bell rolls, its sound
Calls her forth to die,
Beneath the fatal beam she stands
With tears in either eye.

Then on the platform she did stand
The convict then did cry;
The drop it fell, and she was sent
To meet her God on high.

The bolt's withdrawn—her spirits flown,
Its final doom to bear,
May God have mercy on her soul,
Through Christ our Saviour dear.

R. E. Leary, Printer, 19, Strait, Lincoln.

Copy of a broadsheet produced at the time of the trial, telling the story of Eliza Joyce.

The Georgian prison building, Lincoln Castle.

Calcraft placed the noose over her head and pulled the lever which released the trap. It crashed open with a bang and the unfortunate woman dropped below the level of the stage and out of sight of the crowd below. Her body was allowed to hang for the required time, then cut down and buried in the Lucy Tower among the others executed at Lincoln. And so ended the life of Eliza Joyce, who was thirty-one years old and died on 2 August 1844.

Eliza Joyce was born Eliza Chapman in the little village of Butterwick, just outside Boston. It was said that she was 'respectably connected' with relatives in Boston. And it was also said that she had a 'mild not uninteresting appearance'. She married William Joyce in 1840. He was then a market gardener, but had kept a beerhouse in the south part of Boston some six years earlier. William, whose wife had died a little time before, had two children living at home. The eldest was William, who was fifteen, and there was a baby, Emma, who was six months old. In October of the following year little Emma died and Eliza was delivered of her first child to William on New Year's Day 1842. She was called Ann. But Ann did not live long and died on the 21st of the same month.

Fifteen-year-old William suffered with ill health and a Dr Smith was called to see the boy on 13 September 1842 and prescribed some medicine for him. He seemed to improve but on the 16th Eliza went to Mr Smith's chemists shop in Boston and asked to buy some mercury, the local name for arsenic, to poison rats. The chemist was not at all keen to sell her any and suggested she take some 'nux vomica' instead. This was a poison and contained strychnine, but only in low concentration and was sometimes used as a heart stimulant. Strychnine was rarely used by poisoners because of its extremely bitter taste, but was much used as a poison for vermin. Eliza refused the nux vomica however, and said that her husband had told her specifically to buy the white powder. So the chemist prepared 2oz of pure white arsenic for her and wrapped it up in brown paper, carefully labelling it 'Poison'.

The following day Mr Smith, who knew William Joyce, the father, saw him in town and told him about the sale of arsenic to Eliza. William rushed home and returned with the paper packet of arsenic, but there was only 1 ½oz left; the other ½oz could not be found. Eliza said that she had spilt some on the floor. Nevertheless, that day the boy was taken ill with violent stomach pains, vomiting and diarrhoea. His father told the doctor about his wife buying arsenic and the doctor took some of the boy's vomit to have it analysed. The young lad made a partial recovery and in a few days felt rather better. But the doctor was still suspicious that he might have been poisoned and he called in the police. The young boy was subsequently asked to make a statement. He said:

About a month ago I was taken ill, my eyes swelling first and then my legs. Soon afterwards I began to swell all over, but I did not feel any pain at that time. A few days later I became very sick and vomited violently. I continued to be ill until the Friday when I got worse. Between ten and eleven o'clock at night my father went to bed leaving my mother-in-law to sit with me and give me my medicine. At about twelve o'clock she gave me some in a wine glass and a few minutes after taking it I became extremely sick and my heart beat very violently. I continued to be sick at intervals for two or three days afterwards. I told my father that I could not take any more of the medicine because it was making me so bad.

He was asked if he was on good terms with his mother-in-law, and he said, 'Only middling.'

Young William died the following Christmas and Eliza was immediately arrested and charged with administering poison to her stepson on 17 September 1842, because arsenic had been detected in the boy's vomit. She went on trial at the Spring Assizes in Lincoln.

The entrance to Cobb Hall, Lincoln Castle.

But the case was not proceeded with at that time because the boy's name was given on the indictment as William Edward and two witnesses, the boy's father and his grandmother, protested that his name was William only. Because of this mix-up and because the victim must be correctly identified in a serious charge of this nature, the judge stopped the trial. Eliza was formally discharged but was bound over to appear at the next assizes.

In July 1843 Eliza went on trial again. She could not be charged with murder because it could not be proved that the poison she administered in September had actually killed the boy. Therefore, the charge was attempted murder. Eliza admitted buying arsenic but denied giving her stepson any. She said that she spilled some on the floor and scraped it up with a spoon and she might have accidently used the same spoon to give the boy his medicine. In addition, her husband refused to give evidence against her and so it could not be proved that she had ever given the boy arsenic. She was acquitted.

But although William had refused to give evidence against Eliza he was obviously suspicious of her, possibly even afraid that he might be next for the administration of arsenic. He refused to let her remain in the household. It proved impossible for her to find other accommodation and she finished up in the Boston Union – the workhouse – with William paying for her upkeep. But suspicions lingered. If she had administered arsenic to one of William's children, could she have given the same poison to the other, Emma, who died when she was eighteen months old in October 1841? The body was exhumed and the organs were tested, but no arsenic was found.

Even so, the strain had begun to tell on Eliza. She fell ill in the workhouse and was attended by one of the medical officers of the Boston Poor Law Union, Edward Coupland. She became worse and perhaps she felt that she was approaching her death. At all events, the doctor reasoned that she might be in a condition to unburden herself. He encouraged

The roof of Cobb Hall, Lincoln Castle.

The Lucy Tower, Lincoln Castle.

her to talk about her past life and one day in June he asked her about young William and how he had died.

'I gave him arsenic', said Eliza, quite calmly.

The doctor didn't want to put her off by appearing appalled at the admission, so he asked matter of factly, 'How much?'

'About a teaspoonful', replied Eliza.

The medical man nodded and asked about the other child, little Emma. He pointed out that no arsenic had been found in the remains of the child.

'Oh no, sir', said Eliza. 'I did not give her arsenic. I gave her laudanum.'

Laudanum, a dilute solution of morphine, could be sold over the counter in chemists' shops. As will be explained in Chapter Six, it was still being sold without the formality of signing the poisons register as late as 1909. And it was not unknown for parents to give fractious young children small doses of laudanum to quieten them down.

'How much did you give her?' asked Dr Coupland.

'About two teaspoons. I gave about a teaspoon to the baby.'

'The baby? You mean your own child?'

Eliza nodded. She seemed relieved that she had got it off her chest, so to speak. Dr Coupland was so shocked that Eliza had now confessed to murdering three people that he left the subject alone that day. But the next day he returned to it and now Eliza, thinking over what she had done, again seemed quite satisfied that she could tell the doctor about her crimes. And this time she said that she thought she had given little Ann two teaspoons of laudanum and double that amount for the eighteen-month-old Emma. She explained that when she gave the laudanum to Emma the child died very quickly. But with her own child, Ann, she waited until the nurse (presumably the midwife) was out of the room to give the child the laudanum. Ann immediately had convulsions. A Dr Ingram

The top of the Lucy Tower, where felons were buried.

was summoned and he advised putting the baby in a warm bath, but the child died the next day. The doctor gave the reason for death as convulsions, as he had for little Emma, who had died three months before. No post-mortems were carried out at the time.

Dr Coupland also asked her where she had obtained the laudanum and Eliza said, 'Oh, at Mr Smith's shop in Boston.' And when he asked her how much she had bought, she replied, 'Three pennyworth.'

When she was asked why she had killed the young children, she said, 'I don't know, except I thought it was such a troublesome thing to bring a family of children into this troublesome world.' She also said that she had had some words with her husband at the time of Ann's birth, but was generally on middling terms with him. So it is possible she might have suffered depression after Ann's birth. But that hardly explains why she went on to give the poison to young William. It was reported at the time, 'because her mind was so burdened that she could not live, and hoped that, as she confessed, she should be better.'

Eliza Joyce went on trial for the third time on 22 July 1844, before Mr Justice Coltman at the Lincoln Assizes, charged only with the murders of Emma and Ann Joyce. She pleaded guilty and her confession was read in court. In fact, her confession was the sole evidence presented that any murders had been committed. The trial only lasted for an hour and the verdict was guilty of murder. The execution took place eleven days later.

Chapter Four

⊰•◊•⊱

A Shot Too Far

Wyberton is a village lying about two miles to the south-west of Boston. Today most of the village lies to the west of the new A16, which was built to replace the East Lincolnshire Railway line, but the old parish church, St Leodegar, lies to the east of the road. The village takes its name from Wybert, one of the knights of Algar, the Earl of Mercia, who was killed in a battle with the Danes in AD 870. The ruins of Wybert's Castle are about a quarter of a mile to the east of the parish church, though there is very little of it to be seen today. In 1860 the main occupation of the villagers was agriculture. Much of the fertile land around the village, some of it reclaimed from the sea, was used for fattening cattle. However, the cultivation of the woad plant *Isatis tinctoria* was also carried out and would develop later into something of a local industry.

On the evening of Wednesday 24 October 1860, some men were drinking in the Crown and Anchor, a pub situated in Skirbeck Quarter, which was in the area now occupied by the Riverside Industrial Estate, just to the south of the Haven. One of these was Thomas Richardson, a tall muscular man of twenty-six with sandy hair, who was married with two children and lived in Wyberton, near the church. He was a farm labourer, as was James Burrell, a friend who was drinking with him. Also in the party was John King, an older man who had his son George with him.

They all left the pub together at about midnight. There was later some argument about the exact time. The police who visited the pub at 12 a.m. said that the men were not there at that time, but the barmaid said that they did not leave until after twenty past twelve. By the time they left, John King was pretty drunk and had to be helped along by his son. Richardson and Burrell parted from the others when they came to a bridge by a field called Cartwright's Field, and then they were only a few minutes walk from their homes. Burrell lived next door to Richardson in what were presumably terraced farm cottages with only thin walls between them. When Burrell got home and took his boots off downstairs, he could hear Richardson next door. He heard his friend go up the stairs and move about in an upstairs room. And when he was getting into bed he could still hear someone moving upstairs next door.

It was just after 1 a.m. when Alexander McBrian, who was twenty-five, was walking up the road from Frampton, a village to the south of Wyberton. He was a police constable in the North Holland Division of the Lincolnshire Constabulary. He had reached the church when he saw a shadowy figure in a field on the other side of the road. Since it was strange

A view of old cottages at Wyberton.

to find anyone about at that time in the early morning, he crossed over to get a better look at the man. When he got a bit nearer he shouted to him, 'Hello there! Where are you off to this time in the morning?'

The man turned away and said nothing. It looked to the young policeman that the man might have been carrying a gun, so he called out again, 'What are you going to do with that thing?' It must have been pretty obvious that the man was going to do a bit of poaching. The man pulled down his billycock hat over his eyes. The word 'billycock' was used to describe a number of round-brimmed hats, of which the bowler was the most common. The man then turned to face the policeman, raised his gun and fired. He was only a few yards away when he pulled the trigger and the blast almost threw PC McBrian off his feet. The policeman staggered back and the man turned and made off across the field.

PC McBrian tottered across to the first house he saw and pounded on the door. 'Come and help me! I've been shot!'

There was a considerable delay until someone clattered down the stairs and opened the front door. It turned out to be John King, and he was still suffering from the effects of the alcohol he had consumed. He found the policeman slumped by the door. 'Get me a doctor', moaned the injured man.

According to what King later reported, he said to the man, 'Come in a minute and I'll see if I can get my horse and cart out and get you to a doctor.' He turned back into the house and shouted to wake his family to come and help. But when he turned back to the front door he found that the injured man had gone. He went outside and looked around but it was so dark that he could see little in the gloom. In those days they didn't have streetlights. In any case he was not in any fit state to go looking for the injured man, so he went back inside.

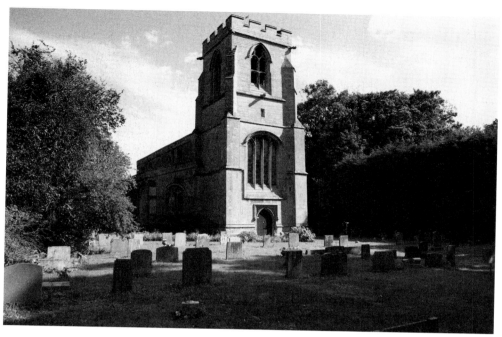

Wyberton Church.

PC McBrian next appeared at the rectory. Here he had more success. The Revd Moore was roused and he got the injured man to come inside. The policeman was in a fainting condition and asked for water. The vicar gave him brandy and water and this revived him a little. He had a fearful gash in his right arm, which was bleeding heavily. The vicar's wife bound up his arm as well as she could and while she was doing this, the vicar asked, 'Who has done this?'

'Oh he is easily to be found. He was only 4yds off me.'

He also asked to be taken to a doctor in Boston and the vicar arranged for his groom to take him in the carriage. During the journey the groom talked to him to try and keep him conscious. He told the groom that the man who had shot him had on a velveteen coat. The groom, under instructions from Revd Moore, first took him to the home of the policeman's superior, Superintendent Manton. When the superintendent was awoken, he immediately sent for Mr Young, the surgeon. And when the wound was examined it was seen that the charge had entered the right arm just below the shoulder joint. McBrian was questioned by the superintendent and reported that the man who had shot him was Thomas Richardson, an individual already known to the police. McBrian was placed in the care of Mr Young and a Dr Adam; later that day the superintendent ordered a search to be made in the area where the assault had taken place. The search party found some wadding on the ground, which had obviously come from a cartridge discharged from a shotgun. The wadding proved to be from part of a newspaper.

The following day the superintendent went to Richardson's house. He wasn't there but the superintendent was armed with a search warrant. He searched the house and found a double-barrelled shotgun and a bag of shot. One of the barrels had been fired but the other had not. He attempted to get the remaining cartridge out of the gun but couldn't, so he took the gun outside and fired it into the ground. This enabled him to get the wadding of the remaining cartridge. It turned out to be made of newspaper. While this was going on, Richardson returned.

'What sort of wadding do you use for your gun?' asked the superintendent, and he showed Richardson the gun he had found.

'Brown paper.'

'Really?' said the policeman, and he showed Richardson the newspaper wadding he had taken from his gun. Richardson made no reply.

Next, Superintendent Manton asked him where he had been the night before and what time he had got home. Richardson said that he had been in the Crown and Anchor and had got home at about 1 a.m. The superintendent took the shot bag away with him and compared the shot with some he had obtained from McBrian's coat. The shot from Richardson's house was mixed shot with two or three sizes, and it corresponded with that taken from the injured man's coat. The next day he went again to Richardson's house and took possession of his shotgun. He then apprehended the man on a charge of shooting with intent to murder.

When charged, Richardson went pale and seemed agitated. Asked if he had anything to say he said, 'I can clear myself of that. I had nothing to do with it.'

He was then taken to the lock-up. On the Saturday he was taken to the bedside of the injured man, in the presence of Major Moore JP. McBrian, who looked very pale, managed to raise himself up in his bed and pointed a shaky finger at Richardson. 'That is the man who shot me', he said.

The constable had lost a lot of blood and in those days blood transfusions were unknown. By the following Wednesday it was obvious that McBrian was sinking fast. A further confrontation was therefore arranged between the dying man and Richardson. McBrian made a further statement. He said, 'This is the man who shot me. I have not the slightest doubt.' And when further questioned, 'I should not have said so if it was not true, and if I am a dying man, he is the man who shot me.' He described his assailant as a tall, stout man with a short neck, broad shoulders and good legs, with breeches or trousers which fitted tight. He had a dark, loose billycock hat on and a coat that reached down to his thighs and stuck out at the bottom.

This seems a pretty positive identification, but it must be remembered that it was a dark, foggy night and McBrian's certainty might well have been coloured by his sight of Richardson after the event, or even by earlier sightings. The fact that he was severely injured and must have been in great pain might also have affected his judgement. However, he stuck to his guns bravely and died the next day, Thursday 1 November, and the investigation now became a murder inquiry.

The question was raised. Did Richardson have time to get home after leaving the pub, go out again and shoot the policeman? A Mrs Sarah Allis, who was a widow living a few minutes walk from the church, heard a shot during the night and looked at her clock. It said two minutes past one. The barmaid at the Crown and Anchor said Richardson left with his friends at twenty minutes past twelve. Burrell said he heard Richardson moving about next door after they reached home but didn't hear him go out again. John King said he also heard the shot only a few minutes after he got home and then shortly after that the

Above A view of the Ship Inn in the 1900s from *The Illustrations Index*. (Courtesy of Lincolnshire County Council)

Right The headline and part of the text from the *Boston Gazette*, 24 November 1860.

THE MURDER AT WYBERTON.

The final investigation into the death of the officer McBrian, took place on Wednesday afternoon last, before J. C. Little, Esq., Coroner.

Capt. Bicknell was present, produced the 'Times' newspaper, and repeated the evidence given before the magistrates, clearly showing that the gun wadding found on the spot where the murder took place and that discovered in the prisoner's gun, were part of the same newspaper.

Edward Frankish deposed; I am one of the County constabulary, and was formerly on the Wyberton and Frampton beat. I know the prisoner, Thos. Richardson. I met him one night in September, 1859, about 11 o'clock. He had a gun in his hand. I asked him what he was doing with a gun at that time of night? He replied, "I don't know that you have anything to do with it." I walked beside him about 200 yards, up to the "Pin Cushion" public-house, in the parish of Wyberton. Just before he went into the house, he said, "I'll be d——d if I don't shoot your b—— brains out before I have done with you." I have frequently met him with a gun in the night.

Robert Hale deposed: I am a member of the County Constabulary, and was on the Wyberton and Frampton beat, on February last, under the superintendence of Mr. Manton. I know the prisoner Richardson well. In February last, Mr Short lost some mutton. I examined the premises of Richardson to see whether I could discover any footmarks corresponding with those on the premises of Mr. Short. About a fortnight afterwards, I met him one night, and he said "you b——, you was one of the men who came about my house looking for footmarks about Short's mutton; I shall do for you before long; so you may look out." I said, "you can't do it level handed, Richardson," and bade him good night.

The Coroner then summed up the evidence; and the jury, after a short consultation, returned a verdict of "Wilful Murder" against Thomas Richardson, who will be tried at Lincoln at the Assizes, commencing on the 5th of December.

wounded policeman turned up at his house. But King's evidence must be suspect because of the state he was in.

Perhaps the most telling evidence came from what we would call today 'forensics'. The chief constable of the county, Captain Bicknell, reported, 'On the 6th of November, I received from Superintendent Manton two separate small packages of pieces of newspaper. I have examined and compared these with a printed copy of *The Times* newspaper of 27 March 1854 and find that the paper comes from a portion of that newspaper.'

The complete newspaper he compared them with came from Peel's Coffee House in London where *The Times* newspapers were regularly filed. The small packages of paper also smelt of sulphur, were stained with gunpowder and had the appearance of having been used as wadding for a gun. Of the two packages of paper, one was picked up at the place where PC McBrian was shot and the other taken from the barrel of the gun belonging to Richardson.

As explained in a recent television programme, *Forensic Casebook* with Matthew Kelly, this was the first time in this country that a gun had been identified as the murder weapon by external evidence. In addition, Joseph Towl, a gunmaker of Boston, compared the samples of shot taken from McBrian's coat with that produced by Superintendent Manton from the bag of shot he took from Richardson's residence and said that they were the same.

At the inquest, which was held at the Ship Inn, PC Edward Frankish told of an incident the year before when he had been patrolling Wyberton at about 11 p.m. He met Thomas Richardson, who had a gun in his hand. He asked him what he was doing with the gun and Richardson told him to mind his own business. He walked with Richardson as far as the Pin Cushion public house where, just before he went into the pub, Richardson said to him, 'I'll be damned if I don't shoot your b----- brains out before I have done with you!' Another policeman, Robert Hale, reported that the previous February there had been a break-in at Mr Short's, the butchers, and he examined Richardson's premises for footmarks to compare with those the thief had made at the butchers shop. About a fortnight later he met Richardson in the street and he said, 'You b------, you was one of the men who came to my house looking for footmarks about Short's mutton. I shall do for you before long, so watch out.'

Thomas Richardson was brought to trial at the Lincolnshire Assizes at Lincoln Castle on Thursday 8 December 1860. The judge pointed out that if the gun had been fired accidently then no one was to blame, but the evidence pointed to the gun being fired deliberately. If the jury were satisfied that it had been fired deliberately, and that Richardson had fired it, then they must being in a verdict of murder against him. The jury took only ten minutes to bring in a verdict of wilful murder against the prisoner. The judge then put on the black cap and sentenced Richardson to death, saying, 'I implore you then to make your peace with the Almighty, for you have no mercy to hope for in this world, and I warn you that you need not expect any.' The execution was fixed for Friday 21 December.

Richardson was much affected by the sentence and on the following Sunday he made a full confession to the governor of the Castle Prison, saying that he had gone home, changed his cap for the billycock hat and taken his shotgun to go poaching. He met McBrian on the road and, fearing detection, he fired at him to make his escape.

The Pin Cushion Inn, Wyberton.

But contrary to what the learned judge had said about Richardson expecting no mercy, a petition of clemency was raised in Boston and supported by several county and borough magistrates. In addition, a letter was sent to the Secretary of State for the Home Office from Dr Clegg of Boston and supported by Mr Malcolm MP. The letter submitted that the crime committed by the prisoner did not amount to homicide of the worst description. There was no malice aforethought and the killing was the result of a sudden impulse and could not possibly have been premeditated. There was no threatening language used by the prisoner, who at the time had the second barrel of his gun 'loaded and capped', and could have used it at any time against the deceased if he had resolved to take his life. But he permitted the injured man to walk away and seek assistance. The letter ended with the hope that the mercy of the Home Secretary would season justice.

On the Wednesday afternoon before the execution, Richardson's wife and relatives were admitted to the castle to take their final leave. The scene was an agonising one, but near the end of the visit the governor announced that he had received a reprieve for the prisoner by telegraph and that his life would be spared. A letter was received the following day from the Home Office commuting the sentence to penal servitude for life.

Chapter Five

⟵⟶◆⟵⟶

Two of a Kind

'Six pennyworth of arsenic, please.'

The chemist looked at the young man standing before him. He looked like a well-set-up young man with an honest face. 'What's your name son?'

'William Hibbins, sir.' And then thinking that he ought to give an account of himself, 'I'm eighteen, an apprentice to Mr Thomas Bacon, who has a whitesmith's business here in Stamford.' (A whitesmith was a person who finished and polished metals, particularly tin plate and galvanised iron.)

'I see', said the chemist, scratching his chin. 'Do you know what he wants it for?'

'He told me he wanted it for hardening iron.' William looked uncomfortable when he said this and he blushed a little, for he didn't really believe that arsenic was used for this purpose.

The chemist's eyebrows shot up and his face took on a look of surprise, since he had never heard of that application before either. But he shrugged his shoulders. 'Have you brought a witness with you?'

William looked puzzled. 'A witness?'

An impatient look crossed the chemist's face. 'I'm not allowed to sell you a poison of that nature, without you signing my arsenic regulations book and bringing someone with you to vouch for you, who must also sign.'

This was early in May 1855, but even as early as that there were strict regulations about the sale of arsenic to members of the public. However, it must be said that there were many preparations at the time containing arsenic, from vermin killers to fly papers and cosmetic preparations, which could be sold freely over the counter. But it wasn't easy to obtain pure arsenic unless you had good reason for using it.

'Oh,' said William, 'I didn't know that.' And he slunk rather shamefacedly from the shop. But when he returned to his master's premises and told him what had happened, Thomas Bacon only laughed. 'Don't worry about it William. I'll get it myself.'

And he did. A week or so later, on 8 May 1855, he went to the same shop in Red Lion Square and asked for an ounce of arsenic, for killing rats. The chemist studied him carefully. 'If you don't want to bother signing the poisons book I can sell you my own preparation, "Vermin Killer" which is very good for killing rats.'

'I've tried that', said Thomas. 'Didn't find it any good. No, I must have pure arsenic.'

Red Lion Street, Stamford, from the Illustrations Index. (Courtesy of Lincolnshire County Council)

The chemist lifted his shoulders. 'Did you bring a witness?' But of course Thomas had forgotten. However, he saw a friend passing in the square and dashed out of the shop. The man agreed to come in and be a witness, and Thomas got his ounce of arsenic.

Thomas Fuller Bacon was thirty years old at the time. He had a house with a workshop attached in the town and he had been married to Martha, who was six years younger than him, for about six years. He came from a wealthy family in Stamford. His father, Nathaniel Bacon, who had also been a whitesmith, had died a few years ago, leaving a great deal of property in the town. His mother, Mrs Ann Bacon, who was sixty at the time, still resided in the large family home in All Saint's Street. Thomas had two elder brothers. William lived with his wife, also Ann, in St Peter's Street and also was a whitesmith, and James lived in London. He also had a sister, Maria Smith, who was married to a farrier and lived in Titchmarsh, Northamptonshire.

It must be said that Thomas did not get on well with his brother William. There was also a good deal of rivalry between the wives, particularly over the matter of having the older Mrs Bacon, who was a very wealthy woman, to Sunday dinner. On Saturday 12 May, William's wife Ann asked her mother-in-law if she would be coming to dinner as usual the next day. But Mrs Bacon said no, she would be dining at home. This was a little white lie, since Thomas had already asked her to come to his house for the meal and she probably didn't want to offend the younger Ann.

The older Mrs Bacon went to church that Sunday morning and then went on to her younger son's house. They were to have soup, a meat course and a pudding. But Mrs Bacon was suddenly taken ill after the soup with sickness and diarrhoea. Thomas and Martha had no servants, but they helped her up to a bedroom and she lay on the bed fully clothed all that afternoon. At about 5 p.m. that afternoon, since his mother was no better, Thomas called in Dr Edward Barber, who was her regular physician. The doctor found his patient still vomiting and very depressed, and after examining her he came to the conclusion that she was suffering from what was called at the time the 'English Cholera'. Cholera was then quite common in many households as the water supply could be contaminated. Dr Barber gave her an opiate pill and some astringent mixture and suggested she be taken home, where she could be looked after by her own servants.

Thomas and Martha took Mrs Bacon home in a sedan chair and she was put to bed. Thomas then went round to see Mary Riley, who lived in one of the houses owned by Mrs Bacon in Protection Street. She had been doing Mrs Bacon's washing for several years and Mrs Riley and Mrs Bacon were very friendly. 'You must come,' he told her, 'the old lady is very bad and I think she will die. You must come and stay with her all night.' Mary quickly put on some outdoor clothes and followed Thomas to All Saint's Street. She found Mrs Bacon in bed and the old lady told Mary that she had not had time to finish her meal before the sickness started. Soon after this, William and his wife Ann arrived and Ann suggested giving the old lady some barley water, but she could not keep it down. After a certain amount of argument between the two wives about what should be done next, it was decided to call in Dr Barber again. He arrived at about 9 p.m, but all he could suggest was more of the same medicine.

Mrs Bacon spent a very disturbed night but she rallied a little the next day. Ann Bacon noticed that Thomas always seemed to be there when she came, and once she noticed that he asked his wife to give his mother something from a bottle on the dressing table containing a whitish mixture. She immediately asked what it was and Thomas told her that his mother had taken some of it already and that it was doing her good. The doctor came periodically, and neighbours came as well. The widow from next door, whom Mrs Bacon had known for twenty years, called later that evening and Mrs Bacon asked her to get into bed with her since she felt so cold. The next day she deteriorated still further and became delirious at times. By the Tuesday the doctor saw that she was sinking and she died later that evening.

Ann noticed that immediately after her mother-in-law's death, Thomas took the bottle from the dressing table. He said that it belonged to him and since his mother would no longer be using it he might as well take it away. Ann also went looking for the rent book which Mrs Bacon kept, since one of William's apprentices collected the rents for the old lady. However, she discovered that Thomas had already taken it and a furious argument developed between them, which went on to include how the property of the late Mrs Bacon should be divided.

Dr Barber remembered that Mrs Bacon had been taken ill in a similar manner the previous March, but she had recovered. He considered that she had been ailing in the interval between that attack and the present one. In the end he put her death down to disease of the brain. There was no inquest and Mrs Bacon's funeral took place on Tuesday 22 May at Great Casterton Church, a village a couple of miles to the north of Stamford and she was buried in the churchyard there.

In January of the following year, Martha had her second child, Sarah Ann. She already had a boy, Edwin Fuller, who was eighteen months old at the time. But Martha suffered severely from depression after the second birth. She became delusional, was sometimes very violent and at times threatened the lives of those nearest and dearest to her. At that time there was no proper treatment available for her and she was sent to an asylum in

London. Mrs Harriet Payne, who was Thomas's aunt and lived with her husband in Mile End, London, came up to Stamford and helped to take Martha down to the St Luke's Lunatic Asylum in London. There she stayed from June until 18 October when it was thought that she was sufficiently recovered to be released. By this time Thomas had moved to London to be near his wife and when she came out he rented a house at No. 4 Four Acre Street, Walworth, near the Elephant and Castle. Thomas got a job with a whitesmith locally, but then just before Christmas he secured a position with a Mr Marriage who had a shop in Reigate.

On the Sunday after Christmas that year, Thomas and Martha went to see his aunt at Mile End. They stayed for the afternoon, but when William Payne, Harriet Payne's husband, came home later that evening he noticed that Martha did not have the children with her. He asked her how she could leave the children like that in an empty house. But Martha replied, 'Uncle, don't you fret about the children; they are happy enough.' While Martha was there she asked Mrs Harriet Monroe, Mrs Payne's married daughter, if she would come over on the Monday afternoon to stop with her while Thomas went to Reigate. Harriet said that she would come over between 4-5 p.m. the next afternoon.

So Harriet presented herself at No. 4 Four Acre Street the next afternoon and knocked on the door of the little terraced house. There was no reply. She knocked repeatedly but no one came to open the door. She thought they must have gone out and went away to return after about an hour. The result was the same. She noticed that the shutters were closed over the windows and there was no sign of life and no lights on inside. Young Harriet tried several times that evening, but she could get no reply to her knocking and eventually she went to her mother's house and told her what had happened. They agreed to try again the next day.

They set out from the Mile End house at 11 a.m. and arrived at Four Acre Street at about 1 p.m.. As they turned the corner they saw Martha coming along the street. In her hand she was holding the rent book with a sovereign on top of it. 'Where have you been all night?' asked Harriet's mother sharply. 'How was it you didn't let my daughter in?'

'I've been in the house all night. But someone came in at the back window and murdered my two children and cut my throat as well.' Now they could see that there was blood on her neck. 'I'm going to pay the rent and tell the landlord all about it.'

The two women stared at her in shock and horror. 'We'll go and look inside first', said Mrs Payne. Martha shrugged her shoulders and they went back to her house. She unlocked the door and they all went in. Martha led the way into the back room. The little boy was sitting in a chair by the fireside. It was an old-fashioned wicker child's chair with a little table in front. His head was resting on the table in front of him and there was a great deal of blood everywhere. Martha repeated what she had said about a man coming through the back window and murdering the children. But Harriet and her mother recoiled from the dreadful scene and soon left the house. All three went to Thomas's brother, James Bacon's, house in Charles Street, Northampton Square. Harriet stayed there and her mother and Martha went on to the police station in Kennington Lane.

They were seen by PC William Cook. Mrs Payne told him that she wanted him to come with them to Four Acre Street as something very serious had taken place there. Martha said nothing at all, but on the way there she repeated the story of the man coming in the window.

The policeman found little Edwin as the others had found him and decided that he was dead. He then asked where the other child was and Mrs Payne said, 'Upstairs in the back room.' There he found young Sarah lying on the floor with her throat cut. Both children had their nightdresses on. 'This is a bad job', said the policeman.

Martha said, 'I didn't do it. A man came in the back window and done it.'

PC Cook examined the sash window in the downstairs back room. The catch was half open but still enough to hold the window closed. No one could have raised the window from outside and the glass was quite sound. There was dust on the inside and outside of the sill. Furthermore, there were no signs of the window having been opened. The policeman made a search of the house and in the front bedroom upstairs he found a woman's nightdress covered in blood and lying on the bed there. He also found an envelope addressed to 'Mr Bacon, Mr Marriage, Ironmonger, Market Place, Reigate'. It had a postage stamp on it and inside was a blank sheet of paper. Martha said the address was in her husband's writing and plainly he had addressed it for her to write to him. PC Cook took Martha back to the police station with Mrs Payne. There Martha was told by the acting inspector that she would be detained regarding the murder of the children and would be taken before a magistrate that afternoon. PC Cook went back to the house that afternoon with the police surgeon, Mr Bushell, who confirmed the death of the children and had them taken to the mortuary. PC Cook also found two bloodstained knives on the table in the back room.

PC Cook was then told to go to Reigate to fetch Thomas, but not to tell him what had happened. He travelled through the night and roused Mr Marriage. His employer didn't know where Thomas was, and he was eventually tracked him down to the Bell Inn, Reigate. It was 1 a.m. when Thomas was roused from his bed, asked if he had an aunt called Mrs Payne, and told that she had reported that something had happened at his home.

When Thomas was delivered to the police station in Kennington Lane he saw Inspector Edward Young, who told him what had happened with his wife and children. He was very much distressed and said immediately that his wife could not have killed her own children. He demanded to see his wife and the children, but was told he could not see her and that his children were dead. He then insisted on going back to Four Acre Street with a police constable to look around. Later he went to see Mrs Payne and her husband. He insisted that Martha would not have killed her own children, but William Payne pointed out that it was very unlikely that anybody else had.

Later that week Inspector Young heard from a constable that Thomas was saying there had been a robbery at his home. He interviewed him and Thomas said that there must have been a break in since some clothes, a watch and £7 in banknotes were missing. The inspector began an investigation and soon found that one of the notes was in the possession of Thomas's brother, James. A search of the brother's house, where Thomas had been living since he returned to London, turned up a pair of fustian trousers which belonged to Thomas and were spotted with blood. But at that time blood analysis was very crude; it wasn't even possible to tell if the blood was animal or human. Nevertheless, suspicions of Thomas were beginning to form in the inspector's mind and when the missing watch was found in the coal-hole at Four Acre Street he considered that Thomas had faked the robbery.

In addition, after examining Martha, Mr Bushell considered that the marks to her throat were self-inflicted. He was also suspicious of the time of death of the two children. When he asked Martha when the break-in had occurred, she immediately said, 'Eight o'clock last night'; referring to Monday night. But the doctor had a feeling that the deaths might have occurred much earlier. Evidence was also gathered from neighbours who were accustomed to hearing the children crying during the day. But nobody had heard the children during all of Monday, even from an early hour when they were used to hearing the crying. Was it possible that the children had been killed sometime on Sunday when Thomas was home?

Developments were also taking place with Martha. During several appearances before the Lambeth magistrates she refused to talk to Thomas and wouldn't even look at him. And then a most sensational development occurred. On 21 January, while Martha was waiting in the cells beneath the Lambeth police court, she asked for pen and paper and wrote the following letter:

Sir, – I must confess that I am an innocent person and he who committed the dreadful deed is my husband, and there was no money in the drawers. He took the little boy downstairs, put him in a chair and there cut his throat; he then went upstairs and cut the little baby's throat.

Signed, Martha Bacon

The letter was immediately taken up to the magistrates. Then Thomas, who was in court to hear the evidence against his wife, was taken into custody and at the police station charged with the murder of his two children.

Thomas and Martha went on trial at the Old Bailey on 11 May 1857. There was a great deal of evidence against Martha; the fact that there was blood on her nightdress and even on her hands and arms, which was present as dried blood when the doctor saw her; the knives in the same room; the preposterous story of the man coming in through the window to kill the children, and the obviously self-inflicted superficial wounds on her neck. And what stood out for most witnesses at the time of the bodies' discovery was her apparent unconcern; one might almost say callousness. Psychiatry was not a developed science at the time but most people recognised a form of insanity when they saw it. Mr Bushell gave it as his opinion: 'That she was not conscious of the act being committed; that is to say, to reflect upon the consequences; she appeared to be indifferent to everything – I did not think she was in her right mind.' The verdict was that she was not guilty, on the grounds of insanity and she was ordered to be detained 'until Her Majesty's pleasure be known.'

There was very little evidence against Thomas. He said he got the blood on his trousers when he cut his finger sharpening a knife. And his faking of a robbery could have been an attempt to support Martha's story. Even Martha's accusation letter was shown to be influenced by outside pressures. At the time she was in the cells at Lambeth police court she was allowed visitors. Among the most persistent were Mary Riley, the washerwoman friend of Thomas's mother, and Mrs Payne. It was suggested at the trial that Mary Riley intimated to Martha that she might be hung if she did not accuse her husband, and why should she be the only one to mount the gallows? During the trial, Thomas was highly distressed, frequently breaking down into tears, and it seems the jury were sympathetic. He was acquitted of murdering his children.

But the publicity that surrounded the case – it was heavily reported in all the national dailies – served to bring to the surface suspicions which had been simmering for years about the death of Thomas's mother in Stamford. Quite a lot of people in the town were firmly convinced that he had poisoned his mother and rumours soon reached the ears of Inspector Young. He asked for an exhumation order for the disinterment of Mrs Bacon's body. At first the Stamford authorities were slow to respond but when the Home Secretary added his name to the request the exhumation then went ahead.

On 6 February 1857 the coffin was raised in the Great Casterton Cemetery in the presence of Professor Taylor, lecturer in Medical Jurisprudence and Chemistry at Guy's Hospital in London, who had been commissioned by the Secretary of State for the Home Office. He took samples from the body for analysis and the inquest was opened at the Plough Inn in the village later the same day. Professor Taylor subsequently confirmed the presence of arsenic in all the tissues he examined. He was able to say that the poison must have been taken or administered to Mrs Bacon while she was living, but he could not say that she had died from arsenic poisoning. The body had degenerated too much for him to be certain that she died from the administration of the poison.

So, effectively, Thomas Bacon cheated the gallows yet again. When his trial went ahead in July 1857 before Mr Justice Erle at Lincoln Assizes, the charge of wilful murder was dropped and he was accused of administering poison with intent to murder. And even when he was found guilty, the judge said that he would not enact the most extreme penalty of the law. Thomas was sentenced to life imprisonment.

Chapter Six

A Fenland Tragedy

'So, you've had your way with me, now you want to get rid of me!'

'I've told you. It's not like that!'

'What is it like then?'

'I've told you. It's my uncle. If you don't go I'll lose my job.'

'And you do everything he says!'

'I can't help it. He's my employer. I'll lose my house as well as my job unless you go. Look, I'm quite prepared to pay for the child.'

'I should think you are, since it's your child.'

'But you've got to leave. You can't stay here.'

The woman, Letitia Key, who was only twenty-four, sank down on the bed and covered her face with her hands. She began weeping. After a brief glance at her, Henry left the bedroom.

The situation was not that uncommon in the Edwardian era. To bear a child out of marriage was a considerable social stigma. Women who had illegitimate children would be regarded as pariahs, especially in rural communities. It was not unknown for young girls who 'fell', as it was termed, to be turned out of their own homes; they would find it very difficult to get jobs to support themselves and would often end up in the workhouse. But the man who impregnated a woman outside of marriage would find it very easy to evade his responsibilities, since there was much less of a stigma attached to him. Conditions were getting a little better in 1909, when this story begins, but old attitudes and opinions prevalent in Victorian times were still held by the older generations.

The man was Henry Idle. He was forty-eight and the foreman of a gang of labourers who worked for his uncle, Mr George Ward, a wealthy farmer in the district. The district was Frampton West, a small and isolated farming community in the Fens a couple of miles west of the large village of Kirton, which is itself some three miles south of Boston. Frampton West was so called because the larger village of Frampton is situated a couple of miles or so to the east of Kirton. Henry's wife had died in November 1907 and in 1909 he had four children still living at home, the eldest being Mabel who was fourteen. Letitia Key was engaged as a live-in housekeeper and to look after the children on 29 August 1908. Henry later claimed that he did not personally engage her and one can only assume that this must have been done by some senior female member of the family, possibly Henry's mother or his aunt, George Ward's wife. Be that as it may,

Kirton Square.

during the nine months or so between his wife's death and engaging Letitia he had had a number of housekeepers. It was suggested to him that there were six but he would only admit to four.

A possible reason for the large number of housekeepers he went through was probably shown when Letitia Key arrived, because within a few weeks he had climbed into her bed. He made it clear later that he did not sleep with her, but that intercourse did take place. One can imagine the scene, with Henry creeping into the bedroom so as not to wake the young child (in those days it was common practice for the mother or whoever was looking after the children to have the smallest child in the bedroom with her) and then creeping out again after a suitable interval to his own bedroom. This carried on until Letitia found herself pregnant and the aforementioned conversation took place. But Henry was adamant. He refused to marry her, but he did offer to support the child. He offered her 1s 6d, which he subsequently raised to 2s 6d a week. At the time he was receiving 15s a week in wages and lived rent-free in the house owned by his uncle. 15s a week would correspond today to a weekly wage of £50 to £60, but it must be remembered that agricultural wages in those days were very low.

Henry said that his uncle had told him that he had a choice. He could stay with Letitia – but if he did he would have to look for another job – or he could tell her to go. Whether this was actually true we do not know, but Henry certainly used it as an excuse for getting rid of her. Letitia did try for several jobs; she put an advertisement in the local newspaper, but she was unsuccessful. Her baby was born on 16 July and christened Grace. After a few days Letitia was up and about and able to carry on with her work, but she did not make preparations to leave and Henry was beginning to get impatient. He questioned her several times about it. Letitia did not say a great deal. She was a quiet, reserved sort of person who kept herself to herself and normally said very little. In conversations with Henry she did not refuse to leave but always maintained that she had nowhere to go. The weeks dragged on. Finally Henry consulted a firm of solicitors in Boston and they agreed to write to Letitia.

High Street,
Kirton.

On the morning of Wednesday 6 October Henry rose early, as farm workers did. When he came downstairs to breakfast he saw Letitia. He asked her if she was having any breakfast, but she declined. Henry looked at her, 'I've been to the solicitors, you know. About you going. And you'll be getting a solicitors' letter.' She said nothing. 'You'll have to go sometime. The sooner the better as far as I'm concerned.'

Letitia still remained silent, looking down at the floor. Then she looked up. 'Will you let me have my weekly wages?'

'Certainly.' To Henry this was a good sign; surely she must be intending to leave, possibly to make a journey. and required money for the fare. He gave her the money and went off to work. At about half past nine that morning young Mabel Idle, who had earlier seen Letitia breastfeeding her baby, saw her now dressed and ready to go out. 'Will you keep an eye on Grace while I'm gone?' Letitia asked. 'I shan't be very long.' The girl said she would.

But Letitia did not return until 11 a.m., and she then went straight up to her room. Mabel followed her upstairs. She saw Letitia sitting down in her room. 'Do you know where my pen is Mabel?'

'I think it's in the red writing case.'

'Would you get it for me?'

Mabel went downstairs to retrieve the writing case and then left Letitia alone to write her letter. Later that morning when the post arrived there was a letter addressed to Letitia. She did not open it but stood looking at it for a while. Then she said, 'Mabel, would you give this to your father when he comes in?'

Henry came in for his meal at about midday. When Mabel gave him the letter he looked at it. 'It's not addressed to me; it's addressed to Miss Key.'

'She asked me to give it to you.'

'I don't care what she asked. It's her letter. She should open it.'

Mabel duly passed the letter back to Letitia, who reluctantly opened it. It read:

THE BOSTON MURDER.

Letitia Key (29) was indicted for having murdered her daughter on October 7th at Frampton West. Mr W. Rylands Adkins, M.P., appeared for the Crown and Mr H. Y. Stanger, K.C., M.P., and Mr T. Hollis Walker for the prisoner.

Mr Adkins said the prisoner became housekeeper to Henry Idle, a farm foreman, who was a widower with a young family, at Frampton West in August last year, and while there had a child, of which Idle was the father. On October 6th she received a letter from Idle's solicitors saying that if she not leave they would take steps to send her away. After receiving this she bought a small bottle of laudanum at a chemist's. In the evening Idle's daughter, aged 14, found her lying on her bed with the baby in her arms. Prisoner told her that the baby was dying, and admitted to a neighbour that she had taken laudanum and given the baby half a teaspoonful. The prisoner's own life was saved, but the child died. Its age was 11 weeks.

Evidence for the prosecution having been called, prisoner entered the witness-box and said that nothing was said about her leaving before the birth of the child. When told of the lawyer's letter, she was upset, as she had nowhere to go to. She gave the baby a little laudanum to keep it from crying. She had no intention of doing it harm, but wanted to keep it quiet " to end her own life." She meant to leave the baby for him to look after. He had always been kind to the child, and apart from the question of her going away to her as well

Prisoner was found guilty of manslaughter. His Lordship said everybody must have considerable sympathy for her. It was very hard upon her to be turned out of the house, for, no matter how much she might have consented, the conduct of her employer in becoming father of that child was as bad as could be. He would deal leniently with her, and sentence her to five months' imprisonment in the second division.

The headline and part of the text from the *Grimsby News*, 5 November 1909.

Boston, 5th October.

Madam, — We have been consulted by your employer, Mr Henry Idle, who informs us that he has given you notice to quit. You decline to leave his premises. Mr Idle has no wish to treat you harshly, but he is quite determined to dispense with your services and we are instructed to inform you that unless you and your child leave his house within seven days from this date our client will have no alternative but to compel you to do so. Our client is ready to meet any just claims which you may have against him and we are willing to see you if you care to call and discuss the matter.

Yours obediently

WAITE, MARRIS and RICE.

A view of old cottages at Kirton.

Letitia read the letter through and then gave it to Henry to read. He glanced through it. Letitia looked at him. 'Are you going to do it?'

'That's what it says, isn't it? You've got seven days.'

Letitia turned abruptly away from him so that he shouldn't see the tears in her eyes and made for the stairs.

'Dinner's ready', said Henry.

Letitia shook her head, not daring herself to speak, and carried on up the stairs. Henry had his meal and then went to work. Mabel waited a while until everybody had finished then she went upstairs to Letitia's room. 'Shall I bring you some food up?'

'No, thank you.'

'Will you have a cup of tea?'

'No. I'm going to lie down, now.'

Mabel could see that the baby was already lying on Letitia's bed.

The afternoon passed quietly and when teatime came one of the younger girls went up to tell Letitia that the meal was ready. Letitia asked the young girl to ask Mabel to come up and undress the baby, and Mabel duly came upstairs. 'Am I to undress the baby?'

'She'll never waken anymore.'

'Is she dead?'

'She's dying.'

The young girl was shocked. 'Why that is cruel of you!' She rushed downstairs and out of the house. Their nearest neighbours, the Harris's, lived one field away but Mabel ran all the way. She saw Mrs Harris and breathlessly poured out her story. Mrs Harris hurriedly put on a coat and together with her son John, came back with Mabel. Together they went to Letitia's bedroom. Letitia was lying on the bed doubled up in pain. The baby was in her arms.

Mrs Harris looked down at the figure on the bed. 'Have you taken anything?'

'Yes, two teaspoonfuls of laudanum', said Letitia in a low voice.

'My God! You haven't given anything to the baby, have you?'

Letitia's face was screwed up in pain. It was sweaty and she was panting heavily. 'Half a teaspoon', she muttered.

A view of Frampton
West.

'Oh my lord! Whatever have you done this for?'

But Letitia only muttered something that Mrs Harris could not hear. However, Mrs Harris was a woman of action; she reached down and took little Grace from her mother's arms. She could see that the child was still breathing. By this time the room was full of people. 'John! Go for a doctor. But do it quickly!' Next she ordered Mabel to fetch her some salt, water and a bucket. She forced the shaking Letitia to drink the salt and water potion and it made her violently sick into the bucket. Mrs Harris thought about giving some of the mixture to the young baby, but then thought that it was perhaps too risky and might do more harm than good. When Letitia had recovered somewhat Mrs Harris asked her, 'Where's the laudanum?' Letitia replied that it was in a bottle on the dressing table. Mrs Harris took it up and noted that it was three parts full.

Henry Idle had arrived home to have his tea before the girls had gone up to see Letitia. Soon after that he had gone out to post some letters, but he hadn't reached the Post Office when he was overtaken by Mrs Airey, one of his servants. She told him that there was trouble at home and that he should go back immediately On the way back they met John Harris. 'I'm going for the doctor', he burst out. 'There's trouble at your home. Miss Key has strangled the child and poisoned herself.'

When Henry arrived at his home and went up to see Letitia, she told him the same story; that she had taken two teaspoonfuls of laudanum and given the baby half a teaspoon. Henry was furious, but had to restrain himself as soon after that the doctor arrived. Dr Witham had come from the nearby village of Kirton. He found the child in a serious condition. He too had heard the rumour that Letitia had strangled the child and had already sent for the police before he arrived at the Idle house. He asked her, 'Have you put anything round the child's neck?' Letitia, who was slowly recovering, repeated what she had already told everyone. He too asked her why she had done it, but she made no reply.

'There's very little we can do for the child, except to keep her warm with hot water bottles. I have another urgent case to attend to so I shan't be able to stay', said Dr Witham as he left.

PC Cowling, who was stationed at Kirton, arrived later and took charge of the bottle of laudanum. There were few in the house who had had much sleep that night. Henry said later that he went into Letitia's bedroom at 3.45 a.m. and found the child dead. Letitia told him that she had died at 3.30 a.m. Dr Witham was informed and he collected the body; later that day he conducted a post-mortem. He reported that the body was well nourished, with no external marks of violence and all the organs were healthy, but the veins of the brain were fuller than usual. He concluded that the child had died of opium poisoning. PC Cowling had received a warrant from his superior, Superintendent Costar of Boston, and he subsequently arrested Letitia on a charge of feloniously and wilfully murdering Grace Key at Frampton West. She was taken to Skirbeck Quarter Police Station.

The inquest was opened on the morning of Friday 8 October. As there was not a convenient pub nearby it was held in the Idles' house. Evidence was given by Mabel Idle, Mrs Harris, Henry Idle and Dr Witham. The doctor was asked by a juryman what the fatal dose of laudanum for a child would be, and he answered that for a child of over three months anything over twenty drops would be fatal. It was also reported at the inquest that on the day the child received the fatal dose Letitia had gone to Kirton in the morning and purchased laudanum at the shop of Mr Shepperson. However, the shopkeeper could not be called because he was on holiday in Ireland, and so the inquest was adjourned for a week.

When Mr Shepperson did appear he confirmed that he had supplied 1oz of laudanum to a woman on that Wednesday morning. He did not ask her name or what she wanted the laudanum for. On being questioned he explained that the law stated that although laudanum was known to be a poison, it could be sold without formalities provided the solution was less than 1 per cent; the solution he sold Miss Key was only 0.75 per cent. He estimated that two and a half teaspoons had been taken from the bottle found on Letitia's dressing table, and that a teaspoon would contain around sixty drops. At the end of the inquest the jury brought in a verdict of wilful murder against Letitia Key. The coroner then signed a warrant committing her to Nottingham Gaol and for trial at the next Lincolnshire Assizes.

The trial took place at the castle in Lincoln on Tuesday 2 November 1909, before Mr Justice Pickford. Letitia was indicted for the wilful murder of her child, Grace Key. She pleaded not guilty. The prosecution was in the hands of Mr W. Rylands Adkin MP and she was defended by Mr H.Y. Stanger KC MP. It came up during the trial that some four years ago Letitia had had an illegitimate child. When all the evidence against her had been presented she went into the witness box. She said that she gave the child some laudanum to keep it from crying. She had no intention of doing it any harm, but wanted to keep it quiet to end her own life. She meant to leave the baby for her father to look after.

After only a short retirement the jury brought in a verdict of manslaughter and the judge said, 'Everybody must have considerable sympathy for the prisoner. It was very hard on her to be turned out of the house, for no matter how much she might have consented, the conduct of her employer in becoming the father of her child was as bad as could be.' The judge said that he would be lenient with her and sentenced her to five months imprisonment.

Chapter Seven

⟹◆⟸

A Brutal Attack

Heckington is one of the largest villages in Lincolnshire. Sitting astride the old road from Boston to Sleaford, it lies halfway between the two. It is a very old village, being mentioned in the Domesday Book, and its present church is the third to stand on the same site as the one mentioned in 1086. However, its main claims to fame today are the annual Heckington Show, which has been held in the village since 1864, and the eight-sailed windmill which stands close to the station. It is said to be the last surviving eight-sailed working mill in the UK, indeed in Europe, and is now open to the public.

It is claimed that Dick Turpin stayed at the Nags Head in the village, and it is known that he was convicted at York Assizes in 1739 of stealing a mare and a foal from Heckington Common. He was found guilty and subsequently hanged. Heckington also takes its place in aeronautical history. In 1811 a James Sadler flew in a hydrogen balloon from Birmingham to Heckington, where it crashed into a tree. It is recorded that he fell out trying to land the balloon but that his co-pilot managed to stay aboard.

In 1833 Heckington was very different to today. There was no railway then and the main road from Boston to Sleaford was little more than a dirt track. At about half past five in the evening of Saturday 9 March, a lone horseman was riding between Heckington and Sleaford. He was John Nicholls, a wine and spirit merchant who lived in Sleaford but had been doing some business in the village and was on his way home. He was about one and a half miles out of the village and though it was getting dark, he spotted what looked like a bundle of clothes by the roadside. As he drew nearer, he saw that it was in fact the body of a man. He dismounted and approached – the man was lying on his back and his face was dreadfully battered. Being of a rather squeamish disposition, Nicholls lifted the man's hand with his riding clop, rather than touching him, to see if he was still alive. The man's hand was floppy and looked to be without life; he had plainly been attacked. Nicholls saw a thick wooden stake which looked as if it had come from a hedge. It was heavily bloodied at one end and had obviously been flung away by the assailant, landing in the nearby hedge. However, it was plain that it was too thick to have come from that particular hedge. The attacker had obviously brought it with him and this made it look like a premeditated assault.

Nicholls decided that he had better go for assistance and he rode back to Heckington to see his friend Gibbs, who was a surgeon in the village. Together the two rode back up the road to where Nicholls had found the body. As they approached they saw a post-chaise come up to the body from the direction of Sleaford. In it were Captain Whyte and the

Revd B. Beridge. The four men held a consultation. It was decided that Nicholls should carry on to Sleaford and inform the chief constable, while Captain White and the Reverend would go on to Heckington and inform the police there. Gibbs stayed behind to examine the body. He quickly determined that the man was quite dead, although the body was still warm. He estimated that the man had not been dead long. The surgeon discovered that the front part of the man's skull was fractured, his nose was broken and his face was severely lacerated. It certainly looked as if the man had sustained a frenzied attack. Gibbs found the stake and he also concluded that it was the weapon used in the attack.

John Robinson, the local constable, arrived from Heckington with a horse and cart and the body was taken to what was called the 'bone house' at Heckington Church; presumably this was the mortuary. Gibbs then remembered that he had seen the murdered man that very afternoon; he had met him in the village and the man had asked him the way to a barber's shop. Gibbs had been going to a house in the village opposite the barbers shop and he had directed the man there. He saw him go into the shop and through the window observed that he was getting a shave. A little later he saw another younger man come up and look through the shop window. After looking for some time the observer moved away, but before the murdered man himself came out.

The inquest on the murdered man was held the following Monday. By this time witnesses had come forward and the identity of the man established. He was William Burbank, a dealer in hare skins, rags and bones etc. At about 2 p.m. that fateful Saturday, he went into the Black Bull in Heckington. He joined a group of men there who were playing four-handed whist. The proprietor knew him and also the men who he had joined; William Taylor, Benjamin Meddler and William Nash. They played together for nearly two hours, then William Burbank came up to the bar to pay for some drinks. He pulled a purse from his pocket and opened it up. The two pints of beer he was paying for cost 6d, but it was quite obvious to the innkeeper, and also to young William Taylor who was standing by the peddler's side, that he had between 20 and 30s in the purse. After he had paid for his drinks he asked the woman behind the bar for the time.

'About four o'clock I think,' answered the innkeeper's wife.

The Nags Head at Heckington.

'I think I'll go and get a shave, then have a wander round the town before I go home.'

And with that he left the pub. After about a quarter of an hour twenty-one-year-old William Taylor also left the pub. As we know, Burbank then met the surgeon in the village and was directed to the barbers shop. The man who had come up and looked through the barbers shop window was later identified by Mr Gibbs as William Taylor.

A little later that afternoon another rag dealer by the name of Isaac Cooke, who lived at Great Hale to the south of Heckington, had come to the windmill to do some business. He was just coming out of the windmill gates when he met William Taylor. He said to him, 'Where are you going this time of night?' (It was then about 5 p.m.)

'I'm going shepherding', Taylor replied.

They exchanged no further words and Taylor set off towards to Sleaford, while Cooke continued on to Heckington. Shortly afterwards he met a razor grinder and his wife, exchanged the time of day with them and soon after that he saw William Burbank, whom he knew. They stopped and chatted and he afterwards said that he thought Burbank was a little tipsy. Then they parted, Burbank going on towards Sleaford and Cooke to Heckington.

The road from Heckington to Sleaford seems to have been fairly busy that Saturday evening, for William Taylor met another man along the way. Mr Hilton was a carpenter in the village, but like a lot of other people at that time he also kept sheep and he was on the road that evening to look after his flock. He met Taylor at sometime after five and the young man asked him if he could tell him where he could get a job shepherding. Hilton said that unfortunately he could not help him and the young man went off. He seemed to be heading for an area known as Father's Close. Hilton knew the place. It was fenced around with quick-growing white thorn and the hedge had recently been plashed (meaning that the hedge had been reduced in both height and width). Because of this there were plenty of large stakes lying around just waiting to be picked up.

William Taylor returned to the Black Bull in Heckington at about 7 p.m. He seemed to have more money on him than before and began buying drinks for everybody. The landlord also observed that Taylor's hands were now clean, as if he recently washed them.

Heckington Windmill.

The headline and part of the text from the *Boston Herald*, 19 March 1833.

He had noticed them particularly because they were very dirty when he had been playing cards earlier in the day.

Taylor was subsequently arrested and at the inquest conducted on the following Monday a confession that he had made was read out:

I was at Brown's house on Saturday last and left at four o'clock. I went to a blacksmith's shop and from there to Father's Close. I went further along the road when the ragman came up and began to call me about the cards. I went on at him and he shoved me into a dike. When I got out he hit me with a stick and knocked me down. I struck him afterwards with a hedge stick which I got from Mr Hilton's hedge. He got up and hit me again with his stick and I knocked him down with the bludgeon and took from his purse two shillings and seven and a half pence. Then I threw the purse across the road and returned to Heckington to Brown's Tom and Jerry shop where I played cards. [A Jerry-shop or a Tom and Jerry shop was an old name for a low-class beerhouse.]

The purse was subsequently found by Joseph Wilson, a cooper living at Heckington, just about where Taylor said he had flung it. The bludgeon was also discovered, this time by Constable Robert Squires. It was a wicked weapon; 4ft long and as thick as a man's arm at the end, with a stout prong which stuck out about 4in from the tip. The green bark had literally been smashed off by the blows and the wood stained a deep crimson from the blood of the murdered man. The constable also searched the prisoner when he was arrested and found 3s 4½d on him.

At the end of the inquest the jury brought in a verdict of wilful murder against William Taylor and he was committed under the coroner's warrant to Lincoln Castle Prison to take his trial at the forthcoming assizes. The trial took place at the Lent Assizes on 15 March 1833 before Mr Justice Bosanquet. The same witnesses appeared and the same evidence was given. When the prosecution case closed the prisoner was asked for his defence, but he merely said, 'I am innocent of the crime.'

This wasn't the end of his defence, however. In his summing up, the judge went through the whole of the evidence, explaining and commenting upon every part which seemed to require it. Then the jury were due to retire, but after a few minutes deliberation among themselves the foreman rose and asked some further questions of Constable Squires.

'Constable, when the prisoner was before the magistrates did he implicate any other persons?'

'Yes, he did.'

Heckington Church.

'Whom did he implicate?'

'He said that he had not murdered William Burbank at all. In fact, he did not even meet him on the road and did not assault him.'

'Did he say who he thought had done it?'

'He said that he had seen the assault taking place and that the man who did it was the razor grinder.'

But the jury were not convinced. The fact that Taylor was seen on the road before Burbank came up pointed to him lying in wait for the man after equipping himself with a stake from a hedge. This indicated the savage attack was premeditated. The jury took just five minutes to return a verdict of guilty of murder and the judge sentenced him to death. Taylor's father, mother and brother visited him in jail the day before the execution, carried out five days after the trial. He was hanged on the roof of Cobb Hall and interred within the castle walls.

Chapter Eight

⟫◆⟪

Mind Your Own Business

'You're a little b------!' shouted Simeon Carter. 'I shall tell your father all about you! Send for him immediately!'

'I shall do no such thing', snapped back Bernard Palfreyman, who was not little and was twenty-six years old. 'My father lives at Gosberton Clough and I'm not sending all the way down there just to satisfy you. You can clear off out of my house!'

There were very few people who spoke to Simeon Carter like that. The older man (he was sixty-three) went very red in the face. He looked round and saw a carving knife on the kitchen table. He picked it up.

'Right, that's it!' He shouted and he rushed across the room with the knife raised in his hand.

Simeon Carter was a self-made man. Born in Eyeworth in Bedfordshire in 1847, he was the son of an agricultural labourer and became one himself when he was only thirteen. But he was ambitious and worked his way up to become an under-gardener, and then in his thirties he moved to Boston. By this time he had married Eliza from Old Bolingbroke and she had born him five daughters. Ten years later he was still living in Boston and had a fried fish shop at 63 Pen Street. Sometime around 1905 he became an ice merchant with premises at 58 Main Ridge, but by 1909 he had retired and had gone to live in Wrangle, a village about eight miles to the north-east of Boston. By now he was a relatively wealthy man, but retirement hung heavy on his hands. Always used to being active he now found little with which to occupy himself. Eventually he took to going across the road from his house in Nut Lane to help out his neighbour, Bernard Palfreyman, who was a farmer.

Bernard had been born in Ecclesall Bierlow, near Sheffield, in 1885. His father John was a schoolmaster who had five children. Bernard was the eldest; then came Alice, Mabel, and then two more sons. John Palfreyman subsequently moved to Gosberton, working at the Clough Schools, and Bernard became a farmer in Wrangle. In 1909 Bernard was single and lived with his unmarried sister Alice, who was two years younger than him. Alice looked after the house for him and helped on the farm.

But there was a clash of personalities between Simeon and Bernard. Simeon was used to getting his own way. He had run two businesses over the years and was used to having people do things as he wanted them done. He found it hard not to criticise the way that Bernard ran the farm, even though he was supposed to be helping him. He also had a

Bede House, Wrangle.

bad temper, as his wife Eliza admitted, and she found that he seemed to be getting worse. He had fallen out with Bernard several times over the past few weeks, but in the latter half of October 1909 he had begun to sleep badly and became extremely short tempered.

It all came to a head one Saturday morning in October. As usual Simeon had hardly slept at all the previous night and before it was light the next morning he was round at Bernard's farm.

'Do you want any help Bernard?'

'No, thank you.'

This seemed to annoy Simeon. Bernard had asked his sister Alice to help him lift a sack of corn and Simeon took exception to this.

'You shouldn't ask a young woman like Alice to lift a heavy sack.'

But Bernard was becoming fed up with Simeon's continual interfering and criticising. 'Look,' he said, 'you mind your own business.'

Simeon's face went red with anger. 'I'll tell your father about you. I'll tell him about the way you abuse your sister like that.'

'You leave my father alone. You've caused enough trouble before, tittle-tattling with your tales to him.'

'You're a liar Bernard!'

This more or less began a row, with both of them accusing the other of various misdemeanours, during which Simeon accused Bernard of being rude to his wife, Eliza. But it fizzled out when Bernard went out to milk the cows. But coming back in again sometime later he found Simeon still there. By this time Eliza herself had arrived.

She had come across from her house some time earlier to ask Simeon to come for his breakfast. But Simeon, who was still seething, said no, he had something to settle with Bernard first.

Eliza could see that her husband was worked up and she knew from experience that it could end in violence. 'Come home with me Simeon and have your breakfast.'

'No! I keep telling you. I'll not go until this is sorted out with Bernard.'

'Do you want me to go and see Bernard? See if I can make it all right?'

'No!' But then Simeon must have thought that perhaps Eliza might be able to calm things down with Bernard and perhaps get him to apologise. 'Well. All right then. But I'll come with you.'

At that moment Bernard walked back into the kitchen. He saw that Simeon was still there and realised by the look on Simeon's face that the older man was still angry and liable to continue the argument. Bernard therefore geared himself up for defending himself. But when he saw that Eliza was there as well he appealed to her. 'Mr Carter says that I have slighted you. I haven't, have I?'

This, of course, put Eliza in a very difficult position. If she agreed with Bernard it would mollify him, but it would upset her husband and after all she had to live with the old man. 'Well,' she said rather doubtfully, 'there was once when you came down to the hayfield and you wouldn't speak to either of us.'

'That was just because I didn't want him there. Always hanging around telling me what to do and criticising me when I didn't do it!'

It was at this stage that Simeon exploded with anger and subsequently picked up the carving knife and rushed at Bernard. The young man retreated round the table, followed by Simeon. But the two women in the room were not idle. As soon as Simeon picked up the knife and rushed at Bernard they followed and grabbed him. Bernard took the opportunity to leave quickly by the back door. The two women struggled with Simeon and it was Alice, the younger and stronger, who managed to wrest the knife from him. Eliza then stood in front of the door to prevent him following Bernard. Simeon stood panting and glowering like a wild animal at bay, but he realised that he could not get past the two women to follow his quarry.

Bernard had gone outside into the yard and was just getting his breath back when a neighbour arrived with a horse. He had come to borrow a horse rake and Bernard helped him to yoke the horse to the rake and then the man then went off. Bernard looked around and not seeing Simeon assumed that the older man had gone home to his breakfast. He picked up a couple of buckets and went to fill them from the well. But if he thought he had got rid of Simeon he was badly mistaken. Suddenly the man appeared behind him, grabbed the long pole with a hook on the end which was used to lower buckets into the well, and hit Bernard over the head with it. Bernard staggered back and fell to the ground. Then, as he was regaining his balance, he saw Simeon drop the pole and fumble in his clothes to withdraw his pocketknife. Bernard scrambled to his feet and rushed away, hotly pursued by Simeon. But although Simeon was imbued with all the energy his fury could give him, he was no match for the younger man who easily outdistanced him. They raced across a field and out on to the village lane. Bernard was able to lose his quarry by turning into a small passageway between two cottages, while the older man rushed past, not noticing that Bernard had gone down there. The younger

Shocking Tragedy at Wrangle.

RETIRED FISH DEALER'S SUICIDE.

ATTACKS A YOUNG FARMER AND THEN SHOOTS HIMSELF.

A MAN WITH "A DREADFUL TEMPER."

A man named Simeon Carter, of Wrangle, formerly of Pen-street, Boston, where he carried on a successful business as a dealer in fried fish, committed suicide on Saturday under tragic circumstances. The deceased, who is described as a man with "a dreadful temper," had been in the habit of assisting a young farmer named Bernard Palfreyman, who lives near. Early on Saturday morning he went to Palfreyman's house, and a quarrel took place. Carter was, it appears, in the opinion of Palfreyman, interfering too much in his affairs, and was told to mind his own business. The deceased picked up a carving knife from the table and ran at Palfreyman with it in his hand, but he was seized by Mrs. Carter and Palfreyman's sister, and the knife taken from him. Palfreyman left the house and Carter followed and struck him on the head with a long pole used in drawing water from the well. Palfreyman ran away with the deceased after him. Carter was again seized by the women, and the young fellow made good his escape. The deceased then went straight to his own house, locked both doors, and shot himself with a small rifle. Upon the door being forced open a minute or two later by P.c. Stephenson, who lives a few yards away, the deceased was found in a dying condition, death taking place almost immediately. The deceased was sitting on the floor with his head on a chair. The rifle was lying between the dead man's knees, and he had evidently placed the muzzle in his mouth and then pulled the trigger. The deceased was 63 years of age.

The headline and part of the text from the *Boston Guardian*, 6 November 1909.

man then crept back towards his own home, going round the back of some cottages and keeping his head below a hedge. He heard the old man puffing back up the road from his vantage point behind the hedge and saw him go past Bernard's house towards his own.

Alice had followed Simeon when he rushed out of the house and saw the two men race away down the lane. Although she was a young woman and fully capable of running after them, her long skirts made it difficult for her to run fast and she soon lost them. She then saw Simeon coming back up the road, his face purple with exertion and fury.

'Have you killed my brother?'

Simeon stopped and leaned on a wall at the side of the lane. 'No,' he puffed, 'I cannot find him.'

'Good.'

Simeon straightened up. 'I'm going to finish it.' And with that he rushed away across the paddock toward his own house.

Alice was not quite sure what he meant or what he proposed to do so she followed him, but not too closely in case he turned on her. He arrived at his own house and went inside. Alice was just behind him and she heard him locking the door. Immediately she was suspicious. 'Mr Carter! Let me in!'

'In a minute,' came the faint reply.

She waited on the doorstep. Suddenly there was sound of a gunshot. It was loud and reverberated all round the village. Alice hurried round to one of the windows looking into the living room. She saw Simeon lying on the floor with his head back resting on the seat of a chair. There was a gun lying between his legs and she could see blood on his head.

Eliza came rushing up and Alice said, 'Simeon's shot himself.'

'Oh Lord! Can we get in?'

'No. He's locked himself in. You'd better go for the police.'

PC Stephenson lived quite close to the Carters and Eliza went immediately to his house, knocked on the door and when the policeman answered it, said, 'Oh come quickly. My husband has shot himself and I can't get in!'

The policeman considered that he needed some support and he went round to the Bede School near the church, where Charles Mendham, the parish council clerk, was teaching. He asked Mendham to come with him and together the two men went to Carter's house. Eliza and Alice were still there together, now with a large proportion of the village, and they explained what had happened. After first looking through the window, PC Stephenson and Charles Mendham tried breaking the door open with their shoulders, but the timbers were too strong. Then Mendham found a heavy sledgehammer lying near the front door and used it to break the lock. Both men went into the house and found Simeon lying in a pool of blood – he died soon after PC Stephenson arrived.

The inquest was held on the following Monday morning in the village at the house of PC Stephenson, with the deputy coroner for the district, Dr R. Tuxford. Identification evidence was provided by Eliza Carter, who also described the incidents at the Palfreyman farm. Her evidence was corroborated by Alice and Bernard, and PC Stephenson and Charles Mendham also gave evidence. The deputy coroner summed up and said that the only point the jury had to consider was whether the deceased man was of sound mind when he committed suicide. He himself did not think that there was any doubt on the subject. He had deliberately made up his mind to shoot himself and went straight home and did it.

But this did not go down too well with the jury. One of them expressed an opinion that the man had lost his temper to such an extent that he hardly knew what he was doing. Another said that he had seen Simeon when he was coming back up the road and he looked more like a wild man than a sane man. After considering their verdict in private the jury found that Carter had committed suicide while temporally insane, and the foreman expressed the jury's sympathy for the relatives.

William Harrison, who had been summoned to serve as a juryman, was fined 10s for not turning up for the inquest.

Chapter Nine

➤◆◄

Death in a Historical Village

The village of Tattershall is about fourteen miles north-west of Boston and on the River Bain, quite close to the confluence with the River Witham. Now a small village, once it was one of the most important settlements in Lincolnshire, not to say in the whole country. This was all down to one man, Ralph Cromwell, who was responsible for building the magnificent castle. The remains of the castle are still there, with the keep magnificently restored. The first castle was begun in 1230 by Robert of Tateshale, who gave his name to the village. The castle then passed through the female line to Maud Bernak, who married the first Ralph Cromwell, but it was their grandson, the third Lord Cromwell, who brought fame to the village.

He fought with Henry V at Agincourt and returned to hold high office in England, but he reached his peak under Henry VI in 1433 when he was appointed Lord High Treasurer of England. He had married an heiress, Margaret Deyncourt, ten years before and had become a very rich man. During his time as treasurer he transformed Tattershall Castle into an imposing residence for himself and his family. Today, Tattershall remains one of the three most important surviving fifteenth-century brick castles in England. Occupation continued until the late seventeenth century but then it fell into ruins, the moats were filled in and much of the castle disappeared. The site was bought by Lord Curzon in 1911 to prevent the ruins being shipped brick-by-brick to America, and after extensive restoration he bequeathed the buildings to the National Trust in 1925. Today, they are open to the public.

Tattershall also had a weekly market from the time of King John, but today sadly all that is left is the Market place with its Market Cross. Today, Tattershall and the neighbouring village of Coningsby are virtually joined together and sit astride the busy A153 road from Horncastle to Sleaford. In 1922 the market was a bustling place and a James William Goose had a house and a butchers shop there. He was a substantial businessman and his house had two servants, Mrs Swain, who came in daily, and Emma Temple, who was nineteen and lived in. Emma had been engaged by Mrs Kate Goose, William's wife, on 26 May 1922, but it wasn't until July the same year that she noticed that young Emma was showing distinct signs of pregnancy. This seems rather surprising, since at that time the girl must have been some seven months into her pregnancy. Emma denied being pregnant at all and Mrs Goose afterwards said that the girl was willing, kind, of a good character and had given every satisfaction, so perhaps she didn't think it was her place to pursue the matter. She might also have been aware that Emma's parents were very poor and relied on the girl's income for support. At all events, she did not try to get rid of the girl. But on 23 August there was

The Market place, Tattershall.

The Market Cross, Tattershall.

Tattershall Castle.

a dance in the village and Emma wanted to go. Mrs Goose remonstrated with her, telling her that she was not really in any fit state to go dancing.

Emma replied, 'You are as bad as all the rest. It has got all over that I am expecting and that I am leaving you.'

Emma had Saturday afternoons off and three weeks later on 9 September she went off as usual after serving the midday meal. She returned at about 9 p.m. Mrs Goose thought she looked rather pale, but the girl said nothing and went up to her room. Mr and Mrs Goose were having their supper in the dining room and when they had finished Emma came down and began clearing away the dishes.

'Don't you want your own supper?' asked Mrs Goose.

'No', replied Emma and carried on clearing the table. But then suddenly a spasm of pain crossed her face. She stood for a moment with her eyes closed, then she left the clearing up and went out of the room. She went down the yard to the privy. It was a dry toilet which was emptied and collected periodically by council workers. Mrs Goose mentioned to her husband that she didn't think Emma looked too good.

'Well you'd better go and see to her hadn't you?'

'I'll give her a few more minutes then I'll go down.'

But Mrs Goose could not contain herself for long and she went to the lavatory at the bottom of the yard and knocked on the door. 'Are you ill, Emma?'

'No', replied the girl in a weak voice.

Mrs Goose went back to the house but she could not settle. She kept telling her husband that she thought the girl was ill, but he didn't seem interested and retired behind his newspaper. Eventually Mrs Goose could stand it no longer. She went down to the privy again and stood outside the door. 'If you're not ill, why don't you come in?'

'I am coming, in a minute', mumbled Emma in a very tired voice.

Mrs Goose stood on one foot and then on the other in an agony of indecision. Then she went back in. But she was back again in a short time, 'You had better come in and go to bed. I am going to wait here until you do.'

There was a short delay and Mrs Goose was just about to hammer on the privy door when it opened slowly and Emma appeared. It was very dark and Mrs Goose could not see her well, but Emma's face looked very pale. When they reached the oil light of the kitchen, Mrs Goose could see that Emma's hands and arms were covered in blood. The girl slumped down into a chair.

Mrs Goose looked at her with concern. 'What have you been doing?'

'Nothing. I'm sure I haven't. I just want to go to bed.'

Mr Goose had left the room by this time, so Mrs Goose, assisted by Mrs Swain, helped the girl up the stairs and into her bed. During the journey up the stairs Emma looked as if she was going to faint and leaned against the wall. Mrs Goose put her arms around her and they continued their slow progress. When they had got the girl into bed she fell asleep almost immediately. The two women came downstairs and Mrs Goose went to find her husband. 'Jim,' she said 'I want you to go and look in the privy.'

The butcher looked at her in astonishment, but when his wife explained that she thought Emma had just given birth, he went. Taking a candle with him he went down the yard and entered the privy. After some searching he eventually found some dark underclothing in the vault of the lavatory and inside was a newly born female child. He laid her carefully on the ground and went for the local doctor. Dr C. W. T. Woods was acting as a locum for the regular doctor, Dr Tyrrell of Coningsby. When he arrived he was taken to the privy and

Horncastle Police Station.

The Fortescue Arms, Tattershall.

shown the child. He only had the light of the candle to see by, but he confirmed that the child was female and that she was dead. He ordered the body to be taken to the kitchen. Mrs Goose had also sent for the local midwife and Mrs Emma Parker was there in the kitchen when Mr Goose carried in the body. By the light in the kitchen it was obvious that a string had been knotted tightly round the child's throat. Mrs Parker had difficulty getting a pair of scissors under the string to cut it because it was so tight.

The doctor went upstairs to see Emma and found her in a small back bedroom. He had to wake her up to examine her and found that her hands, arms and clothes were covered in blood. He quickly determined that she had recently given birth to a baby.

'What did you do with the child?' asked the doctor, but Emma was too distressed to answer. When pressed she broke down in tears, but all she would say was, 'I wish I could die.'

The next day Dr Woods made a post-mortem examination of the child. He determined that it was a full-time baby. Around the neck was a red mark consistent with a string having been tightly wound around it and the windpipe was crushed. On the left side of the neck was a semicircular mark suggesting a knot and the mark had the appearance of having been caused during the short lifetime of the infant. The lips were a natural, healthy colour and the cheeks quite pink. This condition and the pallor of the body below also suggested that the injuries were inflicted whilst the child was alive. There were no other marks of violence on the body. The doctor gave it as his opinion that the child was born alive and that the tying of the cord around its neck was the cause of death.

An inquest was held the following Monday at the Fortescue Arms in Tattershall, conducted by Dr F.J. Walker, the Spilsby coroner. But after hearing evidence from Mrs Kate Goose, Emma Parker, Sergeant Evison and Dr Woods it was adjourned until Emma Temple was in a fit condition to attend. The inquest was resumed on Friday 22 September. Mr W. Clitherow, a solicitor from Horncastle, now appeared for Emma and Superintendent J. Rawding of Spilsby reported that the young woman had been arrested the day before by Inspector T. Wright of Horncastle. When charged, she said, 'I did not do anything to the child.' She was then taken into custody at Horncastle. After hearing further evidence the inquest jury returned a verdict that the cause of death was

Horncastle Police Court.

strangulation by a piece of string around the child's neck and further that the mother 'did feloniously kill the said child.'

The committal proceedings took place at Horncastle Police Court on Tuesday 26 September and after hearing the same evidence presented at the inquest, Emma was committed for trial at the next Lincoln Assizes. The trial took place on Monday 30 October 1922. Mr C.E. Loseby MP prosecuted and Mr E.L. Hadfield appeared for the defence. Emma was charged with the wilful murder of her child. When asked how she pleaded, Emma said, 'I plead guilty, but at the time I didn't know what I was doing.'

The judge replied that he didn't quite know what that plea might be; it was not exactly definite. 'Do you plead guilty to taking the life of the child, but owing to the fact of you just having given birth to it your mind was off its balance?'

'Yes, my lord', Emma replied.

Mr Loseby for the Crown said he was informed that this was the first case in that circuit that had come within the provisions of the new Infanticide Act. It had been recognised that mothers killing babies during periods of depression caused by childbirth or by incompetence in handling babies could not be said to have the premeditation required to substantiate a charge of murder. The new act decreed that a mother who killed her own child of under a year would be charged only with manslaughter.

The judge said that under the new act it was not necessary to put her on trial. It might be thought that she had suffered punishment enough, but the judge also stated that the way he dealt with her should be a deterrent to others in the same position. Emma had already spent five or six weeks in prison awaiting trial and he would therefore pass sentence of four months imprisonment. At the end of that time a nurse would take charge of her, and he hoped the girl would lead a good and useful life.

Chapter Ten

Murder by the River

The oddly named Anton's Gowt is a small village only a couple of miles to the north-west of Boston. It got its name from Sir Anthony Thomas, who was one of a group of people who helped to drain the fenland around Boston in the seventeenth century. 'Gowt' is an old word meaning a sluice or floodgate 'through which the marsh water runs from the reens into the sea', as an ancient records book puts it. The village lies at the junction of the River Witham and the Frith Bank Drain, an artificially made waterway draining the Fens north of Boston, and a lock provides access to the two waterways. The local name for the village is Anton's Gowt Lock. The annual Lincoln to Boston boat race passes through the village and attracts many visitors to the village as crews come from locally and from far afield. A loop line of the Great Northern Railway, which ran from Peterborough to Bawtry, used to pass along the north bank of the River Witham and skirted the village, providing employment for many of the local population. The signal box at Anton's Gowt was the first one passed on the line from Boston to Lincoln, although the nearest stations were Boston and Langrick.

A road runs along the northern bank of the Frith Bank Drain from Cowbridge to Anton's Gowt and on to Langrick. Along the stretch from Cowbridge to Anton's Gowt it was dotted with cottages. In March 1901 one such cottage was occupied by the Kirke family. William Enoch Kirke, the head of the family, was fifty-five years old. He was described as being of stout build, 5ft 11in tall with a round face, and for those days was unusually clean shaven. His wife Ellen was forty-five, a small woman, only 5ft 2in tall, and weighed only 7½st as opposed to her husband's 16st. Her maiden name was Ellen Mountain, the eldest of the eight living children of Mr Mountain. He had been a blacksmith who had worked for many years on the Great Northern Railway and now lived in retirement with his wife in Blue Street, Boston. William and Ellen were married in 1875 in Boston Parish Church. They first of all lived at Kirton, a large village just beyond Wyberton and four or five miles to the south-west of Boston. But it was near enough for them to be able to see the famous Boston 'Stump' of St Botolph's Church. Then William, who had been a farm worker, obtained a job with the Great Northern Railway as a plate layer and they moved, 'flitted' in the local vernacular, to Frith Bank. There they had a nice little house which cost only £5 a year to rent, with some land at the back where William could grow vegetables and potatoes. They could also keep two pigs in a sty which they fed on scraps from their table. They could live quite comfortably.

A view of Anton's Gowt.

Over the years they had seven children, for then large families were common. At the time of this story Herbert, at twenty-five, was the eldest but had emigrated to America. Next came Gertrude, twenty-one, who was in domestic service in Boston. Frederick was eighteen and worked on a local farm, but he went home on Thursdays and Sundays. Then there was Walter, sixteen, who also worked on a farm but lived at home, as did Frank, fourteen, who worked at Mr Higgins' farm as a 'day boy.' Arthur, twelve, and Alfred, seven, were still at school.

William worked for the Great Northern for many years. But about eighteen months before this story begins he developed a bad abscess on the back of his neck. This may well have been a 'collar-stud abscess' in which a small abscess cavity connects with a much larger one via a channel in deeper tissues. At all events, it required an operation on the back of the neck. In those days operations of this kind were done at home and Kirke was attended by a Dr Wrench of Boston. The operation must have been extremely painful, since local anaesthetics were of the most rudimentary kind at this time. Spraying ether on the skin where the evaporation of the solvent produced a cooling sensation was a popular method, but it was not very effective. Since there were no really effective antibiotics, re-infection by bacteria was very common. It was therefore not surprising that William was off work for a considerable time. However, his recovery seemed to be very slow and he did not show any real desire to return to work. Although the Kirkes had three sons who were working, albeit as poorly paid farm workers, they still had two growing boys at home who were not earning anything at all, and medical attention had to be paid for. During the period of William's time off work, Ellen also suffered an illness so there were additional doctor's bills.

William was regarded as normally of a reserved disposition, but it was noticed that he was becoming more surly and irritable and was given to long periods of silence and brooding.

A view of the Frith Bank Drain.

Still, his friends suspected that it was due to his recent medical trauma and he would eventually snap out of it and resume work. This didn't happen and it became the source of much ill feeling between husband and wife. Ellen began to believe that it was just laziness which was keeping William away from work and she began to take him to task about it, inevitably leading to quarrels. Being a practical woman, she realised that if William did not work she herself would have to do something to fill the family coffers.

Henry Robinson and his wife lived on the other side of the Frith Bank Drain. There was only about 200yds between the two properties, but it required a half mile walk to reach the Robinson farm from the Kirkes' house and you had to go over a trestle bridge. Mrs Robinson was expecting a baby and Ellen Kirke made an arrangement with her to go and stay for a week or until the baby was born, to help look after her. The Robinsons would pay her handsomely for doing it. When William heard about it he was furious. He accused her of neglecting him, but she pointed out that they needed the money. Not only that, someone had to stay home to feed the children and look after the livestock. William grumbled, but then he got it into his head that it was all a ruse. Really she was going to live with the Robinsons to be near Henry Robinson. Ellen laughed at this. Henry was a busy farmer and would have no time for flirting with the paid staff. But William would not be convinced. In the end Ellen decided to ignore his protestations and on Tuesday 19 March 1901 she went off to stay with the Robinsons. However, William turned up at the Robinson house almost every day, argued with his wife and told her she should return home. He would sit in the living room while Ellen went about her business looking after Mrs Robinson. William's behaviour was causing discomfort to everyone; Ellen, Henry Robinson and the servant girl Amy Barber. Whenever Ellen had occasion to pass through the room he would start up again.

The Frith Bank Drain Bridge.

On Thursday 21 March 1901, at about 11.30 a.m., young Fred Kirke was passing the Robinson farm when he saw his mother at the garden gate. She beckoned to him and he came over. 'I'm getting fed up with it', she said, and she described how William was continually harassing her at the Robinson house. 'He thinks I'm having an affair with Henry Robinson and I'm not.'

Then William himself came out of the house and went up to the pair, 'What lies is she telling you now?' he shouted. And this was the beginning of yet another argument, but perhaps because of the presence of Fred, William's arguments were more muted and after a time the row fizzled out. Fred continued on to his own home, followed by his father, and Ellen went back to the Robinson house. But later on that day back at the farm where he worked, Fred received a note brought by the servant girl, Amy Barber. It was from his mother and she asked him to call that evening.

When he had finished work at around 6 p.m., when it was getting dark, he washed up in the farm kitchen and walked over to the Robinson house. He could hear his father shouting as he approached the house and he found them all in the large farm kitchen; his mother and father, Henry Robinson and Amy Barber.

'You're not to stay till Tuesday!' shouted his father.

'We've paid her up till next week', protested Henry.

'I don't care! She's got to come home!'

Fred could see that his mother was close to tears. 'Come on Dad. No need to shout. Mum's not doing anything she shouldn't with Mr Robinson. She loves you too much for that.'

There was a silence and it seemed nobody wanted to say anything. Then William muttered, 'She's got a fine way of showing it.'

'Come on Dad. We're both tired. Let's go home.'

'Aren't you staying at the farm tonight?'

'Well I was, but I've changed my mind. They won't mind. But I shall have to be up early tomorrow morning.'

Together they walked home in the darkness, but there was a fitful moon which shone on the water and prevented them from falling in. On the way Fred talked to his father quietly, telling him that his mother couldn't possibly be having an affair, she just wasn't like that. William, who was now close to tears himself, said that he supposed it must be true. 'I'll go and get a job', he promised. 'I'll go down to Higgins' farm on Lady Day and see if he'll sign me on.' Lady Day was 25 March and was the traditional day for farm workers to be hired.

Fred was up early the next morning, but at breakfast William said very little. He had had a bad night. He had tossed and turned, not being able to get off to sleep and when he did sleep he had bad dreams. Then he woke up in a sweat in the early hours and couldn't get off to sleep again. He kept turning it all over in his mind. Nobody seemed to think there was an affair between Ellen and Henry except him. And outwardly they didn't seem to be anything more than mere acquaintances. Was it simply that they were keeping it secret? They were being very clever. They were keeping everybody in the dark and they must be laughing at him behind his back, the way they were fooling him and everybody else. They were laughing at him. He felt himself grow hot with anger.

At 7 a.m. the next morning, a Friday, William was round at the Robinsons' again. He told the servant girl to tell his wife that he wanted to see her. She went upstairs to see Ellen and came back with the message that Ellen could not see him as she was busy with Mrs Robinson. William sat down in the living room again and seethed. Henry came in and William jumped to his feet. 'It's you my wife wants not Mrs Robinson, you know', he said.

Henry Robinson was getting tired of William. He had known the man for nearly ten years and while he had not been a close friend, he had been on good terms with him for a long time. On the other hand he did not want to interfere in a quarrel between man and wife. 'Don't be ridiculous,' he snapped, 'I have no interest in your wife except as a friendly neighbour.' At that Henry left the room.

William sat back down again on the sofa, but he had to wait until 9.30 a.m. for his wife to appear and even then she merely passed through the room without giving him a second glance and went out into the farmyard. William jumped up and followed her. Shortly after, Amy Barber heard a scream coming from the yard. She rushed out and saw William leaning over his wife, who was on the ground. He appeared to be slashing at the back of her neck her with what looked like a knife or an open razor. She could see blood on his hands. The young girl screamed and dashed into the fields for her master. When Henry came into the yard a short time later he saw William still hacking at his wife.

'I'll cut her head off!' he shouted.

'Stop that!' shouted Henry.

William turned and saw the man behind him. He rushed forward brandishing the bloody razor. 'I'll do you next!'

But Henry quickly turned and grabbed a pitchfork which was standing against the wall. He thrust it at William. 'Keep off or I'll run you through!'

William came to an abrupt halt. He looked at Robinson, then at the gleaming tines of the fork pointing towards him. Then he turned and rushed off out of the yard. Some time

The Malcolm Arms,
Anton's Gowt.

A view of Spilsby
Market place with
a statue of Sir John
Franklin.

Spilsby Court House,
now a theatre.

later he turned up at the house of his friend, George Taylor, who was a neighbour and retired blacksmith. Taylor was out in his garden when William arrived, looking very wild and covered in blood. 'I've killed the missus, George', he croaked.

'Why Bill, whatever for?'

'She was having an affair with that Henry Robinson.' He shook his head. 'I get queer in the head sometimes.'

George nodded his head. He suspected it must be something like that which prevented him getting another job. Suddenly William took a bloodstained razor out of his pocket. 'I may as well finish it now', he said, and he put the blade to his throat. But George jumped forward and grabbed the razor from his hand. William struggled to get it back but George's son John, who was the resident blacksmith, rushed up and helped to restrain William. Other men came across the fields to help hold William until the police arrived.

William was taken to the lock-up at Spilsby since it was considered that the murder had taken place in the Spilsby police area. The inquest, however, took place at the Malcolm Arms in Anton's Gowt, and after witnesses were heard, a verdict of wilful murder was brought in against William Kirke. He subsequently appeared before magistrates at Spilsby, a market town famous for being the birthplace of explorer Sir John Franklin, and was committed for trial at the next Lincoln Assizes. He was tried before Mr Justice Wright at Lincoln on Wednesday 3 July. The prosecution was in the hands of Mr Appleby and Mr Lawrence and William was defended by Mr H. Bonsey. At first he pleaded guilty to the charge of murder, but was persuaded to change his plea to not guilty by Mr Bonsey, who put forward a plea of insanity for the prisoner. However, the judge dismissed this in his summing up, saying he could see no evidence that the prisoner was not responsible for his actions. The jury took the hint and after five minutes brought in a verdict of guilty. The judge donned the black cap and sentenced William Kirke to death. Nevertheless, such were the vagaries of the English trial system that the judge was proved wrong; William Kirke was reprieved on the grounds of insanity and sent to Broadmoor.

Chapter Eleven

The Mystery of the Milk Pudding

Wrangle is a village some nine miles to the north-east of Boston. In the Middle Ages it used to be one of the ports, Wrangle Haven, on the north-western side of the Wash, as it was situated on a tidal creek. Indeed, it supplied a ship and eight men when Edward III was raising a navy to invade France in 1359. The creek eventually silted up and the haven was lost, but it left behind arable land and pasture, and the village had a thriving market and the imposing church of St Mary and St Nicholas. But it had another Mary who echoed down the years in a less salubrious manner.

In 1884 there were a number of smallholdings in the village, and one of these was held by William Lefley. In February 1884 he was fifty-nine, having worked all his life on the land and he now owned the cottage he and his wife lived in. He also had a freehold, about eight acres of pasture on which he kept cows. He was a hard-working man, well respected in the village, a member of the Wesleyan Church and a Sunday school teacher. He was also a leading light in the local Gospel Temperance Society. His wife, Mary, was forty-three and the couple had been married for many years, but had no children and lived alone in the cottage with no servants. As far as one could tell relations between them seemed to be average, though Mary did tell one of her neighbours that William had been a brute since Christmas that year. A nephew of William's, William Lister, who had been lodging with them for about five months, said that he had seen nothing of a serious quarrel between them until the night before he left, 1 February. Then there seemed to have been some altercation between them because William refused to sleep with his wife and climbed into bed with his nephew. William Lister soon went off to sleep but when he woke up in the morning his uncle was not there and he assumed that he had gone back to his wife.

Mary would go to Boston once a week to sell butter. On Wednesday 6 February the local carrier from Wrangle, Samuel Spence, picked up Mary Lefley and her husband from outside their cottage at about 9 a.m.. William travelled with them for about half a mile and then walked back to the cottage while Mary went on to Boston. At about half past ten that morning Mary Ann Maidens, a widow who lived in the village, called at William's cottage to borrow a sickle and later Augustus Nesbitt, who was the local carpenter, arrived to discuss the arrangement he had with William to put up 90yds of fencing the following week. William might also have had other visitors since he was engaged in arranging a tea for the Gospel Temperance Society which was to take place on the following day at the nearby Wesleyan Chapel.

Wrangle Church.

We do not know when William had his lunch, but we do know that it included a rice pudding which Mary had made for him. She afterwards said that she had mixed the rice and sugar and had left William to put the milk in and place it in the oven. William said that after he had finished he gave some of the pudding to three of his favourite cats. But very soon afterwards one of them was sick, began frothing at the mouth and lay upon the floor twitching. It very quickly died. A second began to show similar symptoms and it too died. A while later, the third unfortunate animal also succumbed and William began to get worried as he was beginning to feel a bit queasy himself. He got a small basket and put the receptacle which contained the rice pudding in it, then he set off for the local doctor's. The surgery was about a mile away and by the time he got there William was becoming quite ill. He saw the maid, Elizabeth Hill, and asked for the doctor. When she told him that Dr Bubb and his assistant Dr Faskally were both out, he asked to see Dr Bubb's sister. When she fetched her they both found William lying on a pile of straw in a barn. He was in obvious pain, but he was still carrying the basket with the bowl of rice pudding in it. Elizabeth Hill got a blanket and wrapped him in it as he said he was cold. They managed to get him into the house and he placed the basket on the surgery table, saying that he thought that he had been poisoned by the pudding. He then went outside and was violently sick. He was convinced that his wife had poisoned the pudding.

'You must get the doctor as I'm going to die', he kept repeating.

Dr Faskally arrived back at about half past four. He found William in a state of collapse. He was in considerable pain and was weakened because of the continual sickness and purging. He gave the stricken man a restorative but he was immediately sick again. He told the doctor that he thought the pudding was poisoned and Dr Faskally took charge of the basin. John Chapman, a local bricklayer, had come to the surgery for another purpose, but Dr Faskally prevailed upon him to take William home in his cart, saying that he would follow shortly. Chapman helped William into the cart and on the way home he again repeated that the pudding had been poisoned by his wife and that he was going to change his will. 'I think I shall die,' he moaned again.

John Chapman called out to a neighbour, Annie Longden, as he was passing and asked her to come and help him, and together they got William into bed. Another neighbour, Richard Wright, who was the parish clerk, now joined them and when Dr Faskally arrived he told them to get William hot water bottles to help keep him warm. He explained afterwards that he did not expect Lefley to recover and felt that attempting to use an antidote or a stomach pump would not affect the result and would only cause the patient distress.

At about half past six Mary Lefley returned and immediately went upstairs to see her husband. 'What is the matter?' she asked. 'What is all this about?'

William replied in a weak voice, 'You know, my dear, what it is all about. Go down and don't let me see you anymore.'

Mary turned and without another word went back down the stairs. When Dr Faskally came down she asked him what her husband's condition was and if it was true that he had been poisoned. 'I don't think that there is any chance of his recovery', he said. But then he added carefully, 'With respect to the poisoning I haven't made up my mind yet.'

The doctor also told Mary that her husband had accused her of poisoning him. Mary snapped, 'If he has been poisoned he has done it himself. People don't know that he went out the other night and wanted to hang himself. If he has been poisoned I don't know where he could have got it.' But then thinking perhaps that this sounded a bit callous, she also expressed a wish that she hoped he would get better.

Later on, when Richard Wright came downstairs to make William a cup of tea, Mary said, 'I suppose he says he's been poisoned. He hasn't had any poison in the house for years to my knowledge. I also felt very depressed on the way to Boston this morning. I almost got out and came back.'

Mrs Longden was also in the house that evening. She was present when Mary went up to see her husband and later she talked to her downstairs. Mary told her that William had said in the morning that she needn't make him a pudding that day as there was plenty of food in the house. But she told him, 'You always have one and I shall make you one.' She also said that she put the sugar and rice together and left the milk for him to put in. But when she was questioned by Eliza Curl, the wife of the police officer in Wrangle who came to the cottage soon after Mary had got home, she admitted that she made the pudding, 'and put it in the oven for him.' She also said that she made it in a basin, not a dish, and it was to this witness that she said, 'He's been an old brute since Christmas, and if I go upstairs again I'll tell him a thing or two.'

But she didn't go upstairs again and when asked if she would go up and see her husband as he was nearing his end, she turned away. Dr Faskally left at about 8 p.m. and William died about an hour later. Mrs Longden and Richard Wright were with him when he died. When she heard of the death, Mrs Curl got in touch with her husband and he contacted his superior, Superintendent Crawford in Boston. The death was regarded as suspicious and an investigation was begun. The police searched the cottage and came across some

The Assize Court in Lincoln Castle.

white powder which they sent for analysis, but it turned out to be only whiting. Even so, with the number of witnesses they had, the police thought they had a case against Mary Lefley and she was subsequently arrested and charged with murdering her husband. Public feeling was strongly against her; so much so that the morning following the death she went to Boston to consult a solicitor, Mr B.B. Dyer.

On Wednesday 7 May 1884 Mary was tried at the Lincoln Assizes before Mr Justice North. Mr Etherington Smith and Mr Casserley prosecuted and she was defended by Mr Lawrance QC MP. She was dressed in black and had to be helped into the dock as she was suffering from arthritis in her legs. Dr Thomas Stevenson from Guy's Hospital in London had examined organs taken from the body and also the pudding. He said that portions of the pudding contained 135.5 grains of arsenic (between 8-9g) and the lethal dose for a human being was usually two grains of arsenic. The organs also contained substantial amounts of arsenic and he was of the opinion that William Lefley died from the administration of the poison. William Lister was called and he gave evidence of a cask of ale which Mary had ordered and which William said he did not want in the house and they quarrelled about it. Mr Maidens Smith, a potato dealer, recalled a time just before Mary went to Boston when she complained to him about her husband selling some potatoes to a neighbour and she said she wished he was dead and out of the way.

The defence asked the jury to ignore articles which had appeared in the press commenting on the case and which were largely detrimental towards Mary. Mr Lawrance claimed that William committed suicide, adding the arsenic himself to the pudding and then accusing Mary of poisoning him. But this carried little weight with the jury, and when the judge commented unfavourably on her refusal to go up and see her dying husband they took only thirty-five minutes to bring in a verdict of guilty of murder. On being asked if she had anything to say before sentence was passed, Mary said, 'I am not guilty, sir.' But the death sentence was passed and she again said, 'I am not guilty and I never poisoned anybody in my life.'

Her solicitor raised what was called a memorial to the Home Office, pointing out what he thought were weak features of the prosecution case. But the Home Secretary refused to interfere and her execution was fixed for Monday 26 May. Before that day she was visited several times by her four brothers, three sisters and also her mother, who came three or four times. Her brothers and sisters came to say goodbye on Saturday morning and her mother came in the evening. She seemed to be holding up well, but she spent most of Sunday in bed. When she was awoken at 6 a.m. on Monday morning she was in considerable distress, calling out that she was innocent and when the hangman, James Berry from Bradford, arrived in the cell to pinion her she began screaming and had to be carried to the scaffold. The execution was swift, taking barely four minutes.

Right to the very last she claimed she was innocent and many writers have claimed she did not kill her husband. Certainly no poison was found in the house and no evidence was brought to show that she had bought any. Though she might have had a motive to kill William it wasn't very clear what it was. On the other hand, the fact that no poison was found is suspicious in itself. Many households in those days, particularly rural ones, would have rat poison, and the poison in those days contained a considerable amount of arsenic. It would take only a few seconds for Mary to shake half a tin of rat poison into the rice pudding mix, cover it with milk and put it in the oven. Then she could easily conceal the tin or the packet in the basket she was taking to Boston.

However, there is an addendum to this tale. A story is told of a local farmer who, nine years after Mary Lefley's execution, confessed to the murder on his deathbed. He said he was upset with William because he had bested him in some deal. He stole into the house that morning and, finding nobody about, put some rat poison into the rice pudding he found cooking in the oven. Nevertheless, it is by no means unusual for people to confess to murders they have not committed, and this story is probably as fanciful as the one that William poisoned himself. Perhaps we should go with Nigel Gagen in his book *Hanged at Lincoln*, where he says, 'The only certainty in the case seems to be that Mary's guilt was not proved beyond a reasonable doubt.'

Chapter Twelve

❖

A Public Disgrace

Covenham, five and a half miles north-east of Louth, has two parishes adjoining each other making one long village. The northern parish surrounds the Church of St Bartholomew and the southern the Church of St Mary. In 1856 St Bartholomew's had a population of 273 and covered an area of 1,340 acres. Apart from the church there was a Wesleyan Primitive Chapel and a Free Methodist's Chapel. St Mary's was a smaller parish, having a population of 195 and an acreage of 950, but there was a Diocesan School there, built in 1842, which served the Covenham, Fotherby, Little Grimsby, Ludborough and Utterby parishes. Part of St Mary's parish also extended further east across the marsh to the Louth Navigation Canal, and the cluster of houses around the bridge over the canal there was called Austen Fen.

In 1858 there lived in Austen Fen a widow called Mrs Ann Whatmough. She had several children by her late husband but was extremely poor. She was thirty-seven and had a lover, John Plumtree, who was a farm worker. It was almost inevitable in those days, and she soon became pregnant. She told Plumtree about it, but he did not want to marry her and presumably did not want the burden of having to support the child either. He asked her if she could take anything to end the pregnancy and he would give her money to buy what she needed. She promised she would try, but though she later claimed that though she took a 'bucket full of stuff', nothing worked.

There were abortionists around at that time, quite a lot of them in fact, because with no really efficient means of contraception unwanted babies were common. There was even so-called baby farming, in which a woman would agree to take over an unwanted child and find a home for it, or sometimes even going so far as to kill the baby and dispose of the body. But it all cost money, and Ann didn't have much money. Plumtree then suggested that he could do the job for her if she could provide the instrument. She again agreed and procured a piece of wire with a sharp point. He said he would come round at night when everyone had gone to bed. It was the night of 28 June 1858 when he said he would come, but though Ann waited up for him he did not appear, so she used the instrument herself and aborted the foetus. She concealed the body in the house and sent a message to Plumtree by one of her children. He sent a message back that she was to conceal the body and he would come that night and bury it. But though Ann waited all night for him, again he did not turn up.

Ann was in a terrible state, but she knew that she could not rely on John Plumtree so she sent one of her small sons with a message to Lucy Kirk, who was twenty-four and the wife

Covenham St Mary's Church.

of the local blacksmith. Lucy came to see her and Ann explained her predicament. Lucy said she might be able to help her, but she asked for money. Ann had no money to give her but they eventually settled for Ann giving Lucy a pawn ticket for a shawl. Lucy said that her husband would do the job for Ann but he too must be paid and Ann parted with another pawn ticket, this time for a table. Lucy took the body of the child, sewed it up in a piece of linen and put it in a box under her bed. That night her husband, Elisha, carried the body to a nearby field and buried it.

Of course, it was extremely difficult to keep things like that secret in a small community. A neighbour, Susannah Walters, was in Lucy Kirk's house one day soon after when a little girl came with a message from Ann for Lucy. Mrs Walters didn't hear the message but it seemed to annoy Lucy, for she snapped at the little girl, 'Has Mrs Whatmough forgotten what Kirk and I have done for her?' And later still, when Lucy Kirk and Ann Whatmough were at Susannah's house, she overheard Lucy whisper to Ann, 'I have not told Mrs Walters that you have had a child and that Kirk buried it.'

It was in the November of that year that Ann was in the local shop, kept by Sabina Smith, to buy some groceries. She was obviously distressed and Mrs Smith got her a chair to sit on and asked what the matter was.

'I'm really feeling wretched. All my neighbours are against me.'

'Why? Whatever have you done?'

'Well, you may have heard the rumour circulating last June that I had a child. Well I did.' And she related her dealings with John Plumtree.

Sabina Smith did nothing about what Ann had told her, but the situation was obviously preying on Ann's mind. All her neighbours disapproved of what she had done and this

Covenham Methodist Chapel.

St Bartholomew's Church, Covenham.

Austen Fen Bridge.

made her feel all the worse, but it wasn't until the April of the following year that she finally plucked up her courage and went to see Susannah Walters. She sat in a rocking chair in Susannah's kitchen and said that she felt very poorly and she thought that she ought to go to the pauper's infirmary in Hull.

'Why?' asked Susannah.

'I don't think I'm going to get any better. I think I'm going to die.' She looked up at Susannah with tears in her eyes. 'At least I have my poor dead child to meet me at the bar of God.'

But Susannah would have none of that. 'No you won't,' she said sanctimoniously, 'a child which is stillborn has got no soul.'

'But it wasn't stillborn. I murdered it. It made a skimmering noise before it died.'

This was the final straw for Susannah Walters. Soon after Ann had gone she went to the police station in Louth and saw Sergeant Thomas Bazley and told him what Ann had said to her. He asked her to make a statement and then afterwards he went to Elisha Kirk's house. He interviewed both Elisha and his wife Lucy and they both admitted their part in the affair. He asked Elisha where he had buried the body and the blacksmith told him he had buried it in a field belonging to Mrs Robinson. The next day Sergeant Bazley, together with his superintendent and several other policemen, went to the field. Kirk had reported that he had buried the body in a pit in the field, and when the policemen got there they found it was full of water. They drained the pit and discovered the body wrapped in linen a few inches below the bottom of the pit.

The next day Sergeant Bazley took the small bundle to Frederick Tait, a surgeon in Louth, and he carefully examined the body. He said that he imagined it to be the foetus of a seven-month-old child, but it was very badly decomposed, there being scarcely anything left but bones. The sergeant then arrested Ann on a charge of concealing the birth of her child.

But when Ann Whatmough went to trial at the Lincoln Assizes on Monday 25 July 1859, she was charged with murdering her male child on 28 June 1858. However, Mr Roberts, who conducted the prosecution, said that he was surprised that the grand jury had brought in a true bill of wilful murder and that in his opinion the charge should have been concealment of birth. The prisoner had said that the child made a skimmering noise and that she had murdered it with an instrument made by herself. Whether she made these admissions under what he called a 'heated imagination' he could not say, but it was extremely probable and he thought that after hearing the case the jury would be of the opinion that a verdict of concealment of birth would meet the case. He called a number of witnesses and at the end of the case the judge reviewed the evidence. He drew the attention of the jury to the fact that none of the witnesses to whom Ann had confessed had said that she claimed to have murdered the child after it was born. If she killed it before it was delivered naturally at full term, the charge against her could only be for concealment of birth. The jury took the hint and after only a short consultation returned a verdict of concealment of birth. The judge sentenced her to one year's imprisonment. Also indicted at the same time were Elisha and Lucy Kirk. They were charged with aiding and abetting concealment of birth. They both admitted their guilt and the judge gave them six months each.

Chapter Thirteen

Death on the Railway

Sibsey is a village lying on an ancient sand and gravel ridge which runs south from the Wolds and connects the villages of Stickford, Stickney and Sibsey. The ridge has been an ancient trackway for thousands of years for it rises above the Fens on either side and provided a dry walkway across the marsh, which was often flooded in winter. Today the A16 follows the same route south to Boston, Sibsey being only about five miles north of the town. The village was mentioned in the Domesday Book and is thought to be a Saxon settlement. One of its main features is its Trader Mill, a six-sailed mill built in 1877 and still in operation today. A local celebrity was Annie Besant who had been the wife of the vicar, but went to London to take up trade union work and was active in the negotiations with Bryant & May on behalf of the girls making matches who suffered phosphorus poisoning. Another was Arthur Lucan, who was born in the village in 1885 and later became the 'Old Mother Riley' character famous on the stage, films and television.

The Great Northern Railway line from Skegness to Boston crossed, and still does today, the A16 just south of Sibsey, on a level crossing at a place called High Ferry. It was known as Number 9 Crossing and the gatehouse was occupied in 1902 by William Wroot and his wife Harriet. William was sixty years of age, a burly, powerful man who was employed by the railway company as a foreman platelayer. He had been with the railway company for twenty-four years. When William was engaged in looking after the railway track the level crossing gates had to be opened by his wife Harriet, and this was the contract he held with the Great Northern. He was able to rent the house providing his wife was able to open the gates in his absence.

However, their home life was not a happy one. He was described by his employers as an excellent workman but by his family as a man of violent temper. By 1902 both his elder sons had left home. The younger of the two, Harry Wroot, was a farm servant at Wydale Farm, Stickney, only a few miles up the road from Sibsey, but he visited his father only infrequently, no more than two or three times a year. The elder son, John, lived even nearer, only three miles away at Frithville where he too was a farm worker, but he also rarely saw his father. But the one who suffered the most was undoubtedly Harriet. She had endured William's violence for years, until prevailed upon by her sons to leave him.

Their sister, Eliza Jane, had married a young farmer, John Allen, who had a small house in Mount Pleasant on the Boston to Horncastle road (now the B1183). It was north of Frithville and almost on the edge of the parish of Carrington. The house had two

Sibsey Trader Mill.

principal rooms downstairs and two up, with the kitchen being the room nearest the road. Eliza agreed to take in her mother and Harriet, who was sixty-two, moved in on Thursday 11 December 1902. But this arrangement did not suit William. Without Harriet at home he would have to give up his tenancy of the gatehouse at the High Ferry level crossing, and if he couldn't persuade her to come back he would have to look for some alternative accommodation.

William Wroot went to see Harriet at the Allen residence on the following Saturday. He arrived at about 5 p.m. and asked to speak to Harriet alone, but Eliza refused. She had already sent for her brother John, who lived not far away, and had left instructions that should William appear on the doorstep, so to speak, he was to be sent for. The two boys were very much afraid that because of William's violent nature, given the chance he would harm their mother. They, together with Harriet, had already consulted Mr Gane, a solicitor in Boston, with regard to arranging a separation. John Wroot duly arrived and sat in the same room as his mother and father. Wroot pleaded with Harriet to come back to him but she was adamant that she would not. He soon gave up and left before six o'clock, and so did John when he had seen his father off the premises.

On the following Monday William Wroot went to see his superior, Joseph Cooke, the permanent way inspector at Sibsey Station. 'There'll be a chance for Brown to go into the gatehouse', he told him.

'What do you mean, Wroot?'

George Brown was a platelayer like William and lived locally; if the gatehouse became vacant he could have taken it over.

'My wife is gone', said William shortly.

The inspector remembered that Harriet had been ill lately and because of the man's short statement he wondered if she had gone into hospital or even died. 'Has she... er... passed away?'

Wroot frowned. 'No. Nothing like that.' He looked down at the ground. 'My children have fetched her away.'

A view of Sibsey through the trees on the edge of the village.

Inspector Cooke's head jerked up in surprise and he raised his eyebrows, but he said nothing. The silence, however, was pregnant with the unspoken question and William felt it too. He shuffled his feet and looked down at the ground again, but in the end he felt obliged to say something. He muttered in a low voice, 'She's not been a good wife to me.'

The other man felt embarrassed and realised that he didn't want to pursue that line of inquiry. He coughed. 'Right. I'll put that in hand.' And that ended the conversation.

David Capps was a baker with a shop in Sibsey. Later that morning William came into his shop – he looked a little harassed. 'I'd like a small loaf.'

'I'm sorry William, but we're right out of small loaves.' He saw the look of disapproval on the man's face. 'Tell you what I'll do. I'll cut a large loaf in half for you.'

Wroot wrinkled his nose. 'I don't like a loaf cut in half.'

'All right. What about two small twists?'

William thought about it. 'All right', he said. 'I'll take two small twists and I'll have two small cakes as well.'

The baker began wrapping up the bread while William watched him if as to make sure that the baker wrapped up everything he wanted. Eventually he said, 'By the way, save me a small loaf for tomorrow.'

'Right you are, William.'

'After tomorrow I shan't want a deal more of your bread.

Capps frowned, 'What's the reason? Doesn't it suit you?'

'Yes it does, but I shan't want a deal more.' And with that he took up the bread parcel, paid for it and left the shop without another word.

'I can't understand Wroot,' said the baker to his wife later, 'he's been coming in here

A view of the gatehouse at the Sibsey level crossing.

and having a small loaf every morning for the last three months or so and now he says he doesn't want any more.'

'Do you think he's going away or something?'

'I don't know. He's a surly devil anyway.'

Sometime in the early afternoon William asked George Brown to look after the gatehouse for him and open the gates. He said he was going to look at a house to rent and he promised to be back by five o'clock, the time which George would go off duty. George watched him until he disappeared up the line with his heavy overcoat over his arm.

Since Harriet had left William had needed some new accommodation, but it seemed from conversations he had with Harriet that he was hoping she would come back to him, so it may have been that his expressed intention of seeking another place might have simply been a ruse. It was a good three miles from the gatehouse to Eliza Allen's home, but William turned up there at about 4.30 p.m. It was dark by that time and the kitchen was lit by an oil lamp. Only Eliza and her mother were home and both were in the kitchen. Harriet sat by the fire rocking the baby, which was whimpering in her arms. William walked straight into the room and threw his coat on the unoccupied armchair by the fire.

'Roaring again, I see', he said.

Eliza looked at her baby. 'Yes, he's always at it.'

William spoke directly to Harriet. 'I've taken a hut. Are you ready for coming?'

Harriet compressed her lips. 'I shan't be coming.'

'Oh, won't you?'

'No.'

William had gone rather red in the face, but he controlled himself and turned to Eliza. 'What do you say?'

Eliza replied in a tired voice, 'You never seem easy. Let Mother be wherever she will.'

William's lip curled. 'You've been trying to work this now, for two years, haven't you?' he snarled.

'No. I haven't.'

A view of old
cottages at
Frithville.

'You're a liar!'

Eliza shrugged her shoulders. 'Have it your way.'

'I will. Get me a drink of milk.'

For a moment it looked as if Eliza was going to refuse, but eventually she turned away. She went into the scullery which connected with the dairy out the back. While she was there she heard a blow and a scream. She rushed back with the empty glass in her hand. There, by the dim light of the oil lamp and the flickering flames of the fire, she saw her father standing by the side of her mother, who was still sitting in the chair. There was a terrible gash on the top of her head and blood everywhere, even on the wall by the fire. Her mother raised her hand but no sound came. The baby was screaming where it had fallen on the hearthrug. Her father had a small axe in his hand; he stood motionless looking at her. Then he raised the hatchet and Eliza feared that he was going to strike her too, but his hand dropped. She scooped up the screaming child and ran out of the room. Eliza raced across the field outside with the baby still in her arms, to where she could see her husband, screaming, 'Father's killed Mother!'

Her husband told her quickly to go to his brother's house, which was not far away, and then he went into his own house. He found the scene as in some macabre tableau, made all the more horrible because of the low, flickering light. On one side of the fire sat his mother-in-law, her head bowed, with the fearful injury to her skull and covered in blood. On the other sat William Wroot in what was usually regarded as John Allen's armchair, quietly sitting with the axe lying in his lap. It was only a small one, with the shaft about a foot long, but it was spattered with blood.

'You villain!' shouted John. 'What have you done?'

William replied almost conversationally, 'I expected it would come to this, years ago.' Then he said, quite calmly as if nothing had happened, 'Would you get me a drink?'

'No, I won't you bad villain!' said John hotly.

With that William got to his feet, putting the hatchet on the seat behind him. 'There,' he said. 'I'll give you that b-----. It will do to chop kindling with.' And with that he walked out of the house.

Afterwards John Allen said that the hatchet did not belong to him, but he believed that William Wroot did have one like it. This was confirmed by George Brown, who said that it was one which had been broken and had been repaired with a new shaft by Wroot himself. It wasn't one which the foreman platelayer normally used for chopping kindling, however, but he had seen him use it for repairing lamb holes, which were presumably holes in the hedges by the side of the lines through which lambs could stray on to the permanent way. He also said that he hadn't noticed William carrying a hatchet when he left earlier that afternoon. And it was surmised that Wroot had concealed it in the coat he carried over his arm. The foreman platelayer did come back to the gatehouse that night, but it was considerably later than he had said. George Brown was annoyed and taxed him with it, but William was in no mood to say sorry. 'You'll just have to put up with it', he snapped.

But Brown had another bone of contention with him. 'Bill,' he said in an aggrieved tone, 'you'll starve me to death.'

'Why you silly b----! Why didn't you light a fire?'

'I couldn't find the axe to chop some wood.'

Wroot said nothing to this and George Brown went home. Afterwards he said that he never noticed anything different about the man when he saw him that night. This was rather surprising since the older man must have been covered in blood, but perhaps he washed his hands and face in one of the dykes as he walked home, and in the dim light of oil lamps perhaps Brown never noticed the state of Wroot's clothes.

The police arrived at the Allen house later that night. PC Hall, who was stationed at New Bolingbroke, received a telegram that evening sending him to Frithville and PC Wright, who was part of the Horncastle police but was stationed rather nearer at Gypsy Bridge, was also alerted. He was able to get a lift from a neighbour and was the first to arrive. Incidentally, PC Wright was the man who arrested William Kirke, the man who committed a frightful murder not so far away at Anton's Gowt about eighteen months earlier. Later three superintendents, Marshal from Spilsby, Costar from North Holland and Adcock from Boston Borough, arrived accompanied by Sergeant White from Stickney and an immediate search for William Wroot began.

Nothing was seen of the missing man that night, but at eight o'clock the next morning a body was found on the railway line by Sergeant White. It was near the Maude Foster signal box on the East Lincoln line and was identified as being that of William Wroot. Apparently he had committed suicide by kneeling down and placing his head on the line, but the wheel plate of the approaching train had simply hit his head and knocked him off the line, so that the body was hardly damaged apart from the from the head wound responsible for his death. The driver of the train had not even realised that he had hit anything.

Two inquests subsequently took place. The one on Harriet Wroot took place at the White Hart Inn, Mount Pleasant, which was only half a mile from the house where the murder took place. The jury returned a verdict of wilful murder against William Wroot. The inquest on William Wroot himself was held at the Peacock Inn, Sibsey. The jury's verdict was that of *felo de se*; self-murder.

Chapter Fourteen

——◆◆◆——

Matricide

Today Thorpe St Peter is a small village straggling along the road from Spilsby to Wainfleet, lying about two miles to the north-west of that town. It is some twenty miles to the north-east of Boston and has a lovely old church and one pub, the Queen Victoria. In 1849 it had three pubs, the Black Horse, the Queen Victoria and the Three Tuns, and a population of nearly 500. At that time the buried trunks of large trees were often dug up in the parish, demonstrating that it had once formed part of the great forest which had extended eastwards from the Tumby area. It was an agricultural community with 2,880 acres of well-drained marsh and fenland with good grazing and crops of grass and wheat.

Among this peaceful rural community lived a less-than-peaceful family. They lived in that part of the village known as Thorpe Clough. William Ward, the father, was fifty-three and a farmer. He was well known in the area as a drunk and was regularly thrown out of the pubs in the village for disruptive behaviour. His wife Martha was forty-eight at the time and the couple had three children living at home. John was twenty-three in 1849, Jane who was twenty-one and Caroline eighteen; John was described as a small man of slender build, but he made up for his lack of inches by having a larger than usual libido.

When this story begins he had already forced himself on his sister Caroline, who subsequently had a child by him, but then he turned his attentions to the young servant, Susan Boggs. He began to pester her and she protested to her mistress, John's mother Martha. Mrs Ward told John to behave himself and he agreed and Susan was left in peace. But not for long. He soon began to try to get her into bed with him and she again resisted him and again complained to Martha, saying that she would leave the house if he did not desist. When John was called to account again he offered to marry Susan, but she refused him. Perhaps she felt, rightly, that with his roving eye he would not make a very faithful husband, and Mrs Ward agreed with her. Even though he was her son, she felt that he would make a very bad husband for Susan.

John was simmering with resentment after this and when his mother was out of the way he cornered Susan and tried to force his attentions on her. But the girl screamed loudly and this brought Martha running. She managed to separate the two and ordered Susan out of the room. Then, with her face flushed with anger she said to John, 'If you can't keep your hands off the girl I'll throw you out of the house!' This was the start of a furious argument between them, but Martha was adamant. If he didn't behave she would refuse to feed him and see that his father stopped paying him for the work in the fields until he left.

A road sign at Thorpe St Peter.

On Monday 9 April 1849, the morning began badly. John and his mother had another row about Susan which only stopped when he went off to work. Later on that afternoon, about three o'clock, he came back to the house. This time there was only Martha and Susan in the house. He again complained to his mother that she was interfering in his life and this time he took down the shotgun which usually hung over the fireplace on the wall.

'What do you want that for?' snapped his mother.

'I'll either shoot myself or someone else.'

And with that he left the room. He returned after a few minutes and his mother said to him, 'Get off to work!'

'I shan't work ever again!' And off he went again.

Although young Susan was frightened at what he might do, Mrs Ward seemed unconcerned and after a few moments she began dozing in her chair and eventually went off to sleep altogether. Susan sat in a chair nearby and began some sewing. When John finally returned some time later he found his mother fast asleep in her chair. He looked at her for a moment, and then he raised the gun and fired at her head. In the small room the sound was deafening and the poor woman went over backwards in the chair and crashed to the floor. John went over and stood looking down at her. Then he turned to the terrified girl who was cowering in a corner.

'Now she's dead, we can go off together.'

But the terrified girl could only scream, 'You've killed her! You've killed her!' And she made a dash for the door. But John was quicker and stood in the doorway barring her progress.

St Peter's Church at Thorpe St Peter.

A view of Thorpe St Peter.

The Queen Victoria Pub in Thorpe St Peter.

'Come on Susan. Now we can be together. There's no one to stop us now.'

Susan finally came to her senses and realised that she would have to talk to him if she wanted to get out of the room alive or without being raped.

'All right John. But if we are going to go away together, I'll have to go home and get my things.'

At first the young man looked doubtful, but then he said, 'Well all right then. But don't be long.' He stood aside and Susan left the room as quickly as she could. She did go home, but it was to tell her father and brothers to go for the police.

The police finally caught up with John Ward later that day. He was found wandering in the fields in a dazed condition and had made an attempt to cut his own throat. He was taken into custody and his wounds were treated and he was well enough to attend his trial, which took place at the Lincoln Assizes on 17 July before Mr Justice Coleridge. The prosecution was in the hands of Mr Adams and John was defended by Mr Wilmore, who had a difficult job. His defence was eventually that the young man had fired the gun by accident, having no real intention of killing his mother. But the evidence of Susan Boggs showed that he had pointed the gun at his mother while she was asleep, presumably not having the nerve to do it while she was awake and looking at him. The judge summed up against him, showing that he didn't think much of the defence's argument, and the jury agreed with him. They retired for only twenty minutes before bringing in a verdict of guilty of murder and the judge sentenced John Ward to death.

Before the trial and during it, John's father had pestered the police to return the murder weapon to him. When the verdict was finally announced he was allowed to take the gun away, but he then proceeded to hawk it around the castle yard where a crowd was still congregated, proudly showing it to people as a grisly trophy of the murder. The assize court building was, as it is today, in the castle yard. When he was asked by the prison governor, Captain Nicholson, if he wanted to see his son, he said, 'No. I do not want to see the vagabond.'

Because of this behaviour (he was probably drunk at the time) when he and John's sister subsequently turned up at the prison to visit the condemned man just before the execution date, the governor refused to admit him unless he first obtained an order from a magistrate. The old man replied that he had tried to find a magistrate to give him one but could find no one at home. The governor listened to the tearful pleas of John's sister and allowed them in.

The actual execution was attended by large numbers of people. According to the *Lincolnshire Chronicle*, 'Steam boats, railway carriages, wagons, carts, gigs etc. were all wedged full and before the hour of the execution every point commanding a view of the gallows was occupied by a large mob.' The executioner was William Calcraft, who was paid £5 for his services and was allowed to have the condemned man's clothes if he wished. It is not known if he did.

Bibliography

BOOKS

N.V. Gagen, *Hanged at Lincoln (1716-1961)*, private publication, 1998

Adrian Gray, *Crime and Criminals in Victorian Lincolnshire*, Paul Watkins, 1993

Adrian Gray, *Lincolnshire Headlines,* Countryside Books, 1993

Adrian Gray, *Lincolnshire Tales of Mystery and Murder*, Countryside Books, 2004

Adrian Gray, *Tales of Old Lincolnshire*, Countryside Books, 2005

Renée Huggett and Paul Berry, *Daughters of Cain*, George Allen & Unwin Ltd, 1956

John Ketteringham, *Lincolnshire People*, The King's England, 1995

Lincolnshire Villages, Lincolnshire Federation of Women's Institutes, 2002

Jim Murray, *Tealby Gleanings*, Bayons Books, 2000

H.W. Nicholson, *A Short History of Boston*, Guardian Press (Boston), 1977

David Parry, *Lady Poisoners*, The Bluecoat Press, 2001

John Rowland, *Poisoner In The Dock*, Arco Publications, 1960

C.J.S. Thompson, *Poisons And Poisoners*, Harold Shaylor, 1931

C.J.S. Thompson, *Poison Mysteries Unsolved*, Hutchinson & Co., 1937

Stephen Wade, *Lincolnshire Murders*, Sutton Publishing, 2006

Katherine Watson, *Poisoned Lives*, Hambledon & London, 2004

Patrick Wilson, *Murderess*, Michael Joseph, 1971

Neil Wright, *Boston, A Pictorial History*, Phillimore & Co. Ltd, 1994, 2007

NEWSPAPERS AND MAGAZINES

Boston Gazette and Lincolnshire Commercial Advertiser

Boston Guardian and Lincolnshire Independent

Boston, Lincoln, Louth and Spalding Herald

Horncastle News

Lincoln Rutland and Stamford Mercury

Lincolnshire, Boston and Spalding Free Press and South Holland Advertiser

Lincolnshire Chronicle

Lincolnshire Echo

Lincolnshire Gazette

Lincolnshire Times

Louth and North Lincolnshire Advertiser

Louth Standard

Louth Times